WS

CONSCIOUS EVOLUTION

Personal And Planetary Transformation

by
Barry McWaters, Ph.D.

Art
by
Janet Gordon

Institute for the Study of Conscious Evolution
2418 Clement St.
San Francisco, California 94121

ISBN No. 0-87613-071-6
Copyright © 1981

Published by:
New Age Press
3912 Wilshire Blvd.
Los Angeles, California 90010

Printed in the U.S.A.

ii

TABLE OF CONTENTS

Acknowledgements

Who or what can one thank in such an abundant world? I receive so much, in so many ways that I hardly know where to begin. So I'll begin at the top.

I wish first to acknowledge and express my gratitude to the love, wisdom and evolutionary intention of the Universe. By this I am given my life and being in each moment. Within this beneficence there are many who know this limitless source of inspiration and who commit their lives to making it manifest on Earth. To these teachers, I express my deep appreciation.

I am in special debt to G.I. Gurdjieff who left behind a teaching that has inspired my search and provoked in me a remarkably uncomfortable question. What is the meaning of it all?

"What is the sense and significance in general of life on Earth, and in particular of human life?" This is the question that kindled for Gurdjieff his lifelong search for truth and his consequent work of conscious evolution.

Once I had realized that it was extremely unlikely that I would ever actually answer such difficult questions, I somehow found the courage, even the presumption, to write this book. After all, what else have we to do other than to address the most profound questions?

Along the way, many, too numerous to mention, have offered guidance and help. In addition, Patricia Kollings, editor, and George Perkins, publisher, have given much confidence and support. To all of you I send deep thanks.

Special love and gratitude go to my children, Deirdre and Bryan, and to my wife, Susan Campbell. They each have offered my love, joy, confusion and questions—all the elements necessary for the creative process.

THEMATIC OUTLINE

FOREWORD

This is an important book, dealing in simple and direct ways with an important idea: the concept of conscious evolution. This idea has great meaning and power for me. For years it has been a guiding light in my own work. It speaks in a way that is needed in our time to the issues of our meaning as persons and our destiny upon the earth. It can be a seed of vision around which a new orientation to human nature and the structure of society can emerge.

Every culture develops from an implicit worldview that empowers and guides its creativity, its values, and its selection of goals. This worldview is the myth of that culture. By myth, I mean an image that engages us physically, emotionally, mentally and spiritually; such an image is usually beyond mere intellectualization. It speaks to us in powerful, non-verbal ways. It conveys an implicit assumption about what we believe our world to be and how we should act within it. Myths come to seem so natural, so much a part of us, that we act upon them without question.

Today, we are questioning many of our cultural myths and assumptions, particularly those that guide us to relate to each other and to our world in competitive, exploitative and ultimately destructive ways. Such was the myth that allowed America to expand without much regard for social or ecological consequences. These myths, that may have worked for us when we were a pioneer society, do not work in the context of a global society where interrelatedness and interdependence are the rule. Furthermore, myths of materiality that view the earth as a collection of essentially dead matter, devoid of consciousness or purpose, are today being challenged. New sciences are emerging that are revealing the subjective nature of creation and reintroducing the reality of mind and spirit as the determinative principles from which everything else emerges.

Perhaps most eloquently expressive of this shift in mythic images, as described in this book, is the evolution of the "Gaia Hypothesis," the dawning recognition within the physical sciences that perhaps our planet is actually a living organism.

It is in the context of this shift that the idea of conscious evolution emerges as an idea whose time has come. If, for example, the earth is a living being, if consciousness and life are not derivatives from matter but the sources of materiality, if mind is in fact a primary creative principle, then through the development of our consciousness and awareness, we enter into a closer relationship with the guiding and creative forces of the universe. We begin to graduate from a childhood in which we are dependent on the wisdom and actions of others into a young adulthood in which we can begin to take some responsibility for how life unfolds. We can become not just products (or victims) of evolution, but its partners.

As a species, we are terribly irresponsible toward each other and toward our world. We act in ways that damage the connections between us, in ways that limit our potentials for survival rather than expanding our opportunities for creativity. At the heart of the idea of conscious evolution is the idea of responsibility. It is a recognition that I am part of a larger wholeness of life, a "great chain of being" as the Medieval scholars might put it, and that the wellbeing of that wholeness is my responsibility, too. To paraphrase President Kennedy, the idea of conscious evolution suggests that we "ask not what life and our world can do for us, but rather what we can do for life and the potentials within it that seek to emerge into greater wholeness." It is the notion of voluntary history, that we can co-create, together and with the larger orders of consciousness and mind, a future that will be mutually empowering and mutually beneficial.

Conscious evolution is a way of talking about our essential nature. It affirms that we are rooted in and partake of the creative power and essence from which we and the universe are mutually emerging. It demands that we ask ourselves in what way our mutual emergences empower and affect each other.

In the idea of conscious evolution is inherent a promise. I feel there are qualities of beingness that will not come into the forefront of our human experience until we begin to accept a larger sphere of participation in the creative affairs of the whole of life. It is said that we can now see colors more precisely and in greater variation than could our distant ancestors because over the generations human beings have worked with colors, creating subtle hues and shades that have sharpened our ability to see color. In a similar way, there may be perceptions of the universe attuned to its qualities of wholeness and connectedness—mystical perceptions, perhaps, of the oneness of all things—that will evolve for us or sharpen for us as we begin consciously to act with such connections and patterns of interrelatedness. What kind of culture will emerge out of such perceptions?

Much of my work is with people who believe that such a new culture is now emerging. This culture is based on love and wholeness as direct perceptions of reality rather than simply as ethical or moral concepts. For many, this naturally stimulates a desire to predict and outline just what such a culture would be: what kind of society derives from and supports the principles of co-creative participation in the unfoldment and evolution of a living, conscious universe? In what way does the idea of conscious evolution, for example, generate secondary principles for the design and governance of society?

In any transitional period between cultural myths—and that is the nature of the period we are in—there is a tendency to mix old and new principles to create hybrids. Some of this is good, and some of it is confusing and disperses the creative tension through which the new emerges. The point is that we cannot rationally define or plan out just what "conscious evolution" entails, yet. It is not as if we were sitting down in a corporate board room with representatives from Gaia, from other dimensions, from humanity, from nature, and so forth, to draft a blueprint. It is a deeper process than that, emerging from depths beyond the everyday rational mind. The "conscious" part of "conscious evolution" is more than the consciousness we use to pick new clothes or to decide which product line we are going to market next year. It is the participation of a different level of mind, one for which we do not as yet have a good name.

This reminds me of a famous story, which might illustrate this point: a would-be disciple came to a famous spiritual master and proclaimed his intention to become a master, too. Would the teacher accept him as a pupil and instruct him on how to achieve this goal? The master immediately took the disciple to a nearby stream where he threw him in and held him under. Thrashing and struggling for breath, the disciple unsuccessfully tried to break the master's grip until, half-drowned, he was pulled back to the surface. As he was gasping for air, the master told him: "When you want enlightenment as much as you wanted air, you will know what to do."

There is a level of being at which change—or the empowerment to change—ceases to be mental (an idea, a desire, a theory) and becomes instinctive. We tap into a living, spiritual power, a deep source of creativity that is concerned with more than just generating new forms. It is concerned with generating development and the kind of connectedness that can empower inner unfoldment. This is not necessarily an irrational level (though it obeys rules of logic far more complex and holistic than those normally understood by our everyday rational minds), but it is a superrational level. It may be apprehended and worked with by the mind, but its power is not derived from our thinking. So, in the emergence of a new culture, it will be the collective gasping for breath by many people that will trigger the almost instinctive response of power which can then be culturally shaped in whatever way is appropriate.

For some, working with conscious evolution may mean learning how to "tune in" psychically to some other level of beingness and to receive "guidance." This is a difficult issue. The concept of conscious evolution does indeed call us to expand our range of communicativeness, to enter into dialogue, so to speak, with a wider reality and to derive policy from a pool of greater connectedness and interdependence. However, for many people, spiritual guidance is interpreted in too linear a way: it means contacting some specific other beings and allowing them to tell us what to do. Guidance is seen as coming from above down or from the outside in, and neither direction does much to inspire us to touch or understand new depths of ourselves. To gain information is not the same as to increase consciousness; the notion of conscious evolution is not the same as Gaia or spiritual masters or whoever telling us what to do. It is, rather, the work and effort to enlarge our range of understanding and perspective in order to offer ourselves in more holistic ways to the work of playing and creating with our world.

In part, this enlargement is a product of recognizing and living with certain basic principles that relate to the empowering and connective aspects of evolution. This book addresses these principles clearly and concisely. While such principles are only descriptions and not the creative energies themselves, they give us guidelines through which we can align our actions with these energies, thus invoking them into our lives. We must live with the idea of conscious evolution and with the principles underlying it if we are to know it. In the Bible, the verb "to know" is used to suggest sexual or creative, generative knowledge; that is, there is a form of knowing that involves an intimate blending with what is known, from which new life can spring. That kind of knowing does not come from reading a definition. It comes from living with something and becoming part of it, while allowing it to become part of us. It is in this sense that we must come to know the principles that empower us to participate in conscious evolution, by living with them and by living them.

If we are talking about creating an alternative culture, it's very important that we look at some alternative ways of healing the world. If a person has a lifestyle that's creating disease entities that then must be dealt with through surgery, going through surgery may only re-inforce that lifestyle. But if, on the other hand, it can be dealt with through taking on a different lifestyle, it is possible to change much more than the disease entity—it becomes possible to create a different form of life. Through the surgical approach the expertise of the doctor is emphasized; through the alternative approach, the person's own expertise and ability to heal is emphasized.

If we're trying to build a non-violent, holistic culture, the chances are less that we will build that culture if we envision violent and non-holistic ways of getting to it. On the other hand, by invoking these principles of unity, synergy, attunement, alignment and so on, we are saying: "This is a troubled world, but let us try to be like homeopathic elements within it that embody and incarnate the energy of a different world." Thus the effort to understand and embody the principles of conscious evolution has the effect of mutating and altering the whole process of transformation itself.

This book does not provide recipes for conscious evolution; I don't think any book really can, for books speak to only a part of us and not always the part that understands deeply enough the living, experiential qualities of creativity. However, I feel Barry McWaters has done well in describing the principles involved and in relating those principles to conscious, everyday applications. He gives us a place to start.

There are difficult questions around this issue of conscious evolution. What do we mean by consciousness? What do we mean by or expect from evolution? If, as is said in this book, our thoughts create reality, what thoughts? What level of thinking or of mind has this power? What kind of reality is created?

It is a tribute to the idea and power of conscious evolution as a new cultural myth that it can inspire us to explore such questions. It may challenge us with how much we don't know, but it gives us a place to start learning by asking questions. This is the power of this book. It does not attempt to tell us everything, but it opens us to the existence of a new vision of human meaning and destiny. If, indeed, we are now embarking on a new leg of the human journey, one more powerful and creative than anything that has gone before, how good it is to have a place from which to begin.

David Marshall Spangler
April, 1981

Conscious Evolution: A Definition

CONSCIOUS EV O LU TION (kon'shus ev'o-lu shun), n. [L. conscius, to know (of); evolutio, an unfolding: hence, a shared knowledge of and participation in the unfolding of creation.] 1. The emerging potential of human beings to take responsibility, individually and collectively, for a positive future. 2. The process by which an individual human consciousness can transform itself from a state of fear and alienation to one of enlightened cooperation. 3. The capacity of a group to work together synergistically, i.e. to become a functional entity with capabilities beyond the sum of its individual parts. 4. The potential of Humanity to develop a resonant relationship within the parts of itself, with the planet Earth, and with the Cosmos. — to E•VOLVE CON SCIOUS•LY, v.t.

CONSCIOUS EVOLUTION

An Opening

This book in essence is simple. It speaks of human responsibility—the responsibility to actualize our own inherent potentials, such as brilliance, compassion, enlightenment and the ability to serve the evolutionary process. Within the simplicity of a blade of grass lies the complexity of all creation. Within the inevitability of human evolution lies an intricate and profound challenge.

What is conscious evolution? It is a perplexing problem and a possible process. It is an opportunity that we may or may not avail ourselves of. It is our chance to play a role in evolution. This book intends to disturb our sleep and awaken our potential—a difficult task to be sure. But there it is, an apparent paradox—a simple book with complex notions and a difficult task.

PART I

JUST NOW

Our Moment in Evolution

Chapter 1: **A Global Vision**
The evolution of Humanity is imbued with new meaning when viewed as an experiment in the development of planetary self-consciousness.

Chapter 2: **What On Earth Is Conscious Evolution?**
Conscious evolution is that latter evolutionary phase in which a developing being becomes conscious of itself, aware of the process in which it is involved, and begins voluntarily to participate in the work of evolution.

Chapter 3: **We Are What We Think**
We can now choose our dominant modes of thought and perception and thereby influence the reality we experience.

CHAPTER 1

A GLOBAL VISION

We, all the people alive today, are the generation born when Gaia, our living planetary system, is undergoing an organic shift from unconscious to conscious evolution. We are the first generation to be aware that we, individually and collectively, can and must be co-creators of the future.

People in all walks of life now have the opportunity to participate in the emergence of a new age—a time of awakening and rebirth in the long and majestic process of planetary evolution.

**We can voluntarily actualize our potential
to discover and nurture transformative
thoughts and beliefs, and thereby influence the quality of life on Planet Earth.
We can participate in conscious evolution.**

This book goes round and around the central theme of conscious evolution, approaching it from many angles, repeating
this idea and related seminal concepts numerous times. The
attempt is *to communicate.* The aim is twofold: *to encourage
deeper personal meaning through conscious participation in a
larger reality;* and *to seed the idea of the planet as a living,
intelligent organism in evolutionary process.* This broad perspective, it is hoped, will help us go beyond the 'homocentric'
bias that has been painfully omnipresent in modern Western
culture. This bias, which places the planet at the service of
Humanity, has already resulted in damage to atmospheric
conditions as well as to many plant and animal species in all
parts of the world. It seems evident, therefore, that this limited
perspective is an inversion of the great evolutionary plan which
ultimately calls for a cooperative venture among all conscious
beings.

 **The evolution of Humanity is imbued with
new meaning when viewed as an experiment in the development of planetary self-
consciousness.**

Humanity may well have been called forth to serve Gaia,
rather than vice versa. Our right understanding of this relationship may, in fact, be the key to a new age.

What does this mean? All around us we hear the idea that we
are entering a new age, the Age of Aquarius, the dawning of a
new level of human consciousness and human activity. While

descriptions of this new age seem to vary widely depending on point of view, there are some key elements that are widely accepted. It is clearly an age of scientific inquiry and development wherein new potentials in the outer dimensions of human activity are unfolding. Humans now have the capacity to communicate with any part of the planet almost instantaneously; the possibility of widespread health and physical wellbeing; and the potential to leave the planet and colonize space. These are exciting possibilities.

In the inner dimensions, there are indications that new levels of psychic ability and varied states of consciousness are becoming more accessible to the individual. Research into ESP or Psi phenomena is on the increase. Centers are springing up that teach such skills as clairvoyance, auric reading and healing. In addition, there is serious inquiry into the nature of collective, conscious entities such as the esoteric group, the soul of the nation-state or culture, and the consciousness of Humanity as one living being, the Human Being. More exciting possibilities!

Conscious Evolution as a Choice

Should all this talk be seen as another mirage leading us into even greater illusion than we currently find ourselves? Or should we take it all seriously and place our attention on the task of co-creating a new reality? Is there a middle ground? These are real and vital questions. Perhaps we can begin by examining the motivational forces within the individual. What is it that prompts our frighteningly realistic concerns for the present and our "unreasonable" hopes for the future.

Generally, two distinct yet complementary sources of motivations move us to action. One springs from deficiency and despair, the other from inspiration and hope. Recognizing the pain and distress of our world today, we are moved to respond. Our time is one of acute crisis. People are forced to pay attention to the future by a myriad of survival issues, such as diminishing natural resources, environmental pollution, widespread starvation, and increasing violence and crime. Also, we have developed means of warfare that are so frightening that it has become self-evident that an entirely different quality of human consciousness must be realized in order to insure the continuation of human evolution. People feel within themselves a great poverty, a lack, a sense that something more is needed. This urgency pushes us to search for a new truth, a new way of being that will appease this feeling, that will bring at least some sense of fulfillment.

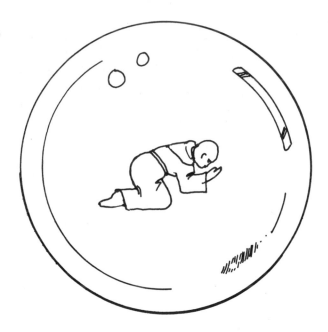

The second source of motivation is, fortunately, more positive. We are drawn, we are called by something deep within ourselves toward exciting potentials. On the one hand, there are tremendous developments in the scientific/technological realm. We are awed by the continual unfolding of our power to manipulate and control outer reality—as if anything were possible. Already we are able to leave the planet, and soon we will be founding new worlds within the solar system, the galaxy, and the universe. The potential suggested by the eruption of new knowledge and new capacity are unlimited. We are intrigued and attracted. We are excited and urged from within to sacrifice the old modes of living and being, and to invite the unknown.

Simultaneously, we are attracted to an array of inner potentials. Many have experienced a new quality of being and consciousness that excites our creativity, that compels us to search even more deeply within ourselves—not because anything is wrong, but rather because we have now tasted what can be. Again we are called to go beyond the old forms, to sacrifice the old ways of being, to enlighten ourselves to a new reality.

Some have suggested that this search for self-realization is arch-narcissism—this navel-gazing and all that. But it's too late for such naivete. We already know better. While it is true that unchecked self-interest can only result in social conflict and ecological rape, it is also true that real compassion can only be discovered deep within the Self. We have not yet seen what can result when self-inquiry penetrates deeply enough to tap into the universal need for conscious evolution.

How shall we progress, then, from individualistic selfishness to enlightened service? The egoistic demand of self-interest is potent indeed, and those who deny its force are often besieged by nightmares, constipation, phantoms, fears, and other strange forms of ill health. Thus we are well advised to use this narcissistic impulse as a motivation to begin the search. For, in fact, what we wish for ourselves turns out to be exactly what is needed for the whole. As we penetrate within, we eventually discover the Universe. This is the beneficent dupe.

We are delightfully tricked to believe that we personally will profit from our quest,

but, in the end, we discover our common
humanity, our love for Mother Earth, and
our intimate need to participate in the
living Universe.

The widespread consciousness movement that began with
harsh encounter, and then progressed to the self-regarding
humanistic ethic, led directly to the search for deeper, transpersonal dimensions of consciousness. And now we spill right
into the Universe. We find that we are awakened to care for the
whole, not from a superficial altruism, but rather from a deep
sense of unity. How then to serve this new understanding?
What values to live by, what images to hold in mind, what
actions to take?

Conscious Evolution as a Unifying Principle

What is the deeper meaning of this individual transformation to which so much attention has been given? Many people
today are experiencing a positive personal life, rich inter-
personal relationships, and a deep spiritual contact. We have
what we came for. Yet the question arises forcefully: Where
does it lead me? What now? Is it all really just for myself?

Clearly, a need from within calls for our attention at this
moment in evolutionary time. The call is to serve the well-being
of the living planet Earth, Gaia. (Gaia is the earth goddess of
the ancient Greeks who regarded the planet as a living
spiritual being.) The call is to enter into a holistic consciousness from which all peoples, all forms of life, all manner of
universal manifestation are seen as interdependent aspects of
one truth.

What can help us toward this realization? In this time of
diversity and conflict, we need to discover a powerful unifying

principle—something around which we can begin to relate our
ideas and activities. Both G.I. Gurdjieff (Ouspensky, 1949)
and Sri Aurobindo (Satprem, 1974), two of the great savants
of this century, have offered us the unifying concept of
conscious evolution.

We, Humanity, are at that point in planetary evolution
where we (for the first time) can begin consciously to *know* that
we are in evolutionary process. We are part of it; we are the
expression of a long and gradual transformation—an inex-
plicable metamorphosis. We see we are guided from within or
above, as it were, yet we also see that our beliefs, thoughts and
actions co-create the reality we experience.

We begin to realize that we are evolution.

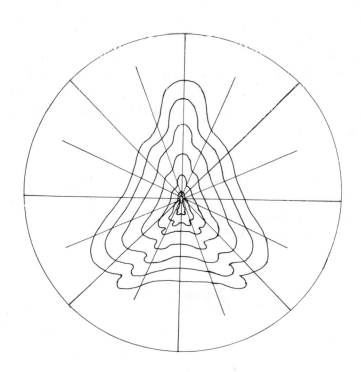

For thousands of years the potential for self-initiated personal transformation has been studied. Esoteric sciences concerned with this miraculous process have developed in various parts of the world. However, only recently have we become infatuated with a scientific perspective that studies and outlines the evolutionary history of the planet and Humanity. With Darwin, the idea of progressive, evolutionary development became widely accepted. Since then, we of the West have viewed all this wondrous manifestation as a mechanical process, the result of accidental mutation.

Just now, we are beginning to combine the scientific notion of evolutionary mechanics with the esoteric notion of a consciously-directed experiment. With a deepened understanding of ourselves and our place in the larger process of evolution, we now come to the threshold of discovering our role in relation to the planet. We now begin to enact the great evolutionary experiment wherein the youthful, often troubled, self-consciousness of Gaia (that's us, Humanity) finally unites with her ancient intuitive wisdom. The task is great; our capacity modest. It is clear that we need an increasingly deeper understanding of evolution so that we may begin to take our part as well as possible. Good luck to us then in the cosmic play of conscious evolution!

 We now begin to enact the great evolutionary experiment wherein the youthful, self-consciousness of Gaia finally unites with her ancient intuitive wisdom.

CHAPTER 2

WHAT ON EARTH IS CONSCIOUS EVOLUTION?

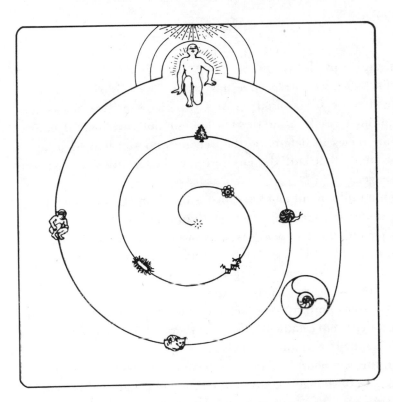

Surveying the long process of planetary evolution will lead toward an understanding of conscious evolution. Different perspectives about evolution appear and disappear, each with its own bias, each with its own unique contribution. The two most notably distinct perspectives are the Western scientific and the Eastern metaphysical. While in some ways these vantage points are polar opposites, they do share the vision of the gradual development of physical life forms over billions of years. They also mutually rejoice in the emergence of human consciousness as a remarkable evolutionary event. And yet, the how and the why of all this remains an issue of considerable debate.

Science and Metaphysics

The scientific perspective has regarded the intricate web of life that we see around us and experience within us as the combined result of natural selection and accident. Chance alone seems to determine the arising and survival of unique mutations that suit the environment better than the genetic lineage.

Of a million-odd monkeys, just a few happen to be born with super-tails—longer and stronger than the rest. Now, while the owners of these super-tails may well have been judged as unfashionable, it was (so the story goes) just these socially misfit creatures that managed best to escape their predators and live to bear offspring. And so on, and so on for many generations until at long last very long tails became quite the rage. The environment, then, rather efficiently selects the "well-suited" mutant for survival.

In this way more and more well-adapted organisms evolve in response to changes in environmental conditions—which are, it is said, also the result of fortuitous circumstance. Thus we of the Western mind have conjured up a picture of an undirected, mechanical evolution resulting in a variety of highly complex life forms such as the human being with its inexplicably large brain.

While the Darwinian perspective is rather uninspiring, it is undeniable that the breadth and precision of related research have contributed profoundly to our emerging understanding. Biological evolutionists have probed deeply into the subtleties of evolutionary process and have thereby provided us with a sophistication of detail undreamt of by metaphysical philosophers. Dobzhanski, for example, in the classic work *Evolution* (1977), notes that in the attempt to discover an exact evolutionary lineage some 100,000 marine species have been identified and described.

In her research into the origin and development of cellular life (Marguelles, 1970), Microbiologist Lynn Marguelles demonstrates how two billion years ago separate tiny living organisms may have joined together symbiotically to create the first complex cell—a new type of living being. This unified "eukaryotic cell" was unique in possessing a definite nucleus, a center, and also unique in its high level integration of differentiated functions performed by the newly united parts. Almost all forms that we consider life today are descendants of this early example of evolutionary transformation. However, inspired as this research may be, survival and accident are still the implied motivational forces.

The Eastern metaphysical, or esoteric, perspective, on the other hand, sees a purposeful Divine Will that inspires and directs the course of evolution. This Will is constantly initiating new experiments in the discovery and development of more highly organized and more conscious forms of life. The *intention* of this Higher Will is the creation of entities, or beings, who eventually will be able to serve consciously the larger process of universal evolution.

> Evolution is progressive adaptation to the environment and it is also a movement of consciousness upward in the scale of being. It is the response to the call of Logos, of God. It is the Purpose behind the Plan. It is God's drawing of his creation back to Himself.
>
> (*The Rainbow Bridge*, 1975:14)

Something deep in our nature is touched by this perspective. At the same time, many questions are left unanswered. The esoteric perspective offers only one piece of the puzzle.

Nonetheless, with the inclusion of the notions of intention and higher purpose, many questions unexplained by biological evolution can be examined in a new light. For example, according to Blavatsky (1915) the universe is, and has been since the creation, comprised of seven basic levels of consciousness or being. As humans, we experience daily the physical, emotional and mental planes, with occasional glimpses of the fourth, intuitional plane. The three higher spiritual levels are, with rare exception, inaccessible to us except as the result of long years of inner practice.

From this perspective, organisms, evolving in time, pass through and express the dominant qualities of each level as they progress toward the highest.

Humanity, rather than stumbling endlessly through time, is now being called to ascend to the next intuitional level of consciousness.

This is the plane that is said to connect the higher and the lower, heaven and earth. Herein we know our divine nature and our human predicament. Herein we will discover our true calling. As we continue to evolve, the very nature of our experience as well as the planetary function of our consciousness will become qualitatively different. We have the potential to transcend our current limitations and to serve a higher purpose. Imbuing the process of evolution with meaning and depth, this perspective speaks to our deepest intuitive sense of universal coherence.

How to find a synthesis, a way of including both the science of the West and the metaphysics of the East? Responses have already been posed, yet we have had difficulty hearing. Three-time Nobel Prize winner Albert Szent-Gyorgyi (1974), after years of research, finds himself confronted with a pervasive "drive in living matter to perfect itself." Physicist Lancelot Law Whyte (1965) announces the discovery of "internal factors in evolution." Each organism, according to Whyte, demonstrates *an inherent tendency* to internally organize itself into more and more sophisticated patterns. This tendency is so omnipresent and self-evident in evolutionary development that it has been invisible to our perception, conditioned as we have been to look only for external causation. This inherent patterning is visible in the beauty of a rose, the complexity of the human being and in the emerging integration of a planetary consciousness. Whyte recognizes this inner drive, this spontaneous intention, to be of co-equal importance with the force of natural selection. Thus, an entirely new scientific vision of the evolutionary process may be forthcoming.

We see a wonderful convergence here, a wedding of internal and external intention—a higher consciousness calling forth new life forms, while the life forms themselves reach toward the light in self-developmental quest.

Our Evolutionary Childhood

Drawing upon this synthetic perspective, we can now take a look at planetary evolution. Some four and a half billion years ago the Earth appeared in space. Through the condensation of gases (it is explained), suddenly (by cosmic time) a solid mass appears, caught in a vortex of cosmic forces (that just happened to be about.) First there was no earth, then there was —number one unexplained miracle. Perhaps Gaia herself decided to materialize just there and set up housekeeping with the Sun. Who knows? In any case, it was a magnificent and important event. A birth.

A billion years later we note the initial stirrings of unicellular life. First there was no life, then there was—number two unexplained miracle. From whence came this undulating life? Was it from the sea of inconscience, or was it called to manifest, to set the stage for a magnificent journey into the light? No one knows. In any case we, the living beings of Earth, were born.

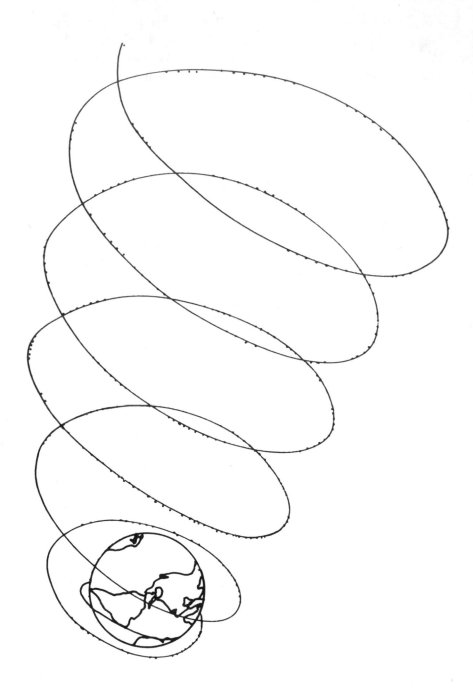

Another billion and a half years pass; a growing attraction appears—perhaps from loneliness or ennui, perhaps from excitement or love. New relationships are sought. Tiny little beings are finding ways to get together, projects to work on, entities to join. This is the origin of the eukaryotic cell—number three unexplained miracle. Who called these little fellows together? Was it simply a matter of coincidence or were they summoned by an inner voice to move forward into our evolutionary potential?

Some time later another wave of attraction sweeps through the being of Gaia. In a great urge for company, cellular division, mitosis appears. Multicellular life becomes the dominant theme—number four unexplained miracle. The dance of life becomes more complex and more interesting as a myriad of species begin to spring forth into the light of consciousness.

Long eons pass silently, full of fervent activity. Three major strands of life have identified themselves: the fungi, who absorb nourishment right through their very skin; the plants who feed on the sun; and the animals who have developed a system of punctures through which they can ingest and eliminate a variety of types of encapsulated energy. And just from this last unusual strain, let us say about ten million years ago, the trouble appears. Humanity is born—a new type of consciousness emerges—number five unexplained miracle. Beings are now moving about the biosphere and altering the environment to meet their own interests and needs. A remarkable event indeed. Did we ask permission? Or were we called to experiment, to try out something new?

So here we are today, in the midst of all this evolving, wondering what to do next now that we see a bit of how we have come to be, and now that we realize that how we shall be in the future is determined to some degree by the choices we make today. We are so very young that perhaps not too much can be expected.

If we imagine that Gaia is in her mid-life with another four and a half billion years to go, then we, Humanity, with our ten million years since birth, are equivalent to a two-month-old baby.

Not too much can be asked, and yet we are up against it. Gaia calls 'wake my child, the time is nigh.'

We are so, so young and yet we are called to open our eyes to the potentials of life, consciousness and service all at once. We wish to remain at the breast, but that is of the past. The age of conscious evolution is upon us. How shall we rise to the occasion?

Conscious Evolutionary Development

Although we as a species are exceptionally young, just learning self-direction, we have nonetheless an adult-like task before us. Viewing Gaia as a planet in mid-life, it seems appropriate that she would, just about now, be developing her capacity for self-consciousness. This newly discovered self-awareness will be quite distinct from her ancient self-regulative wisdom. This new capacity will be more superficial, more flashy, more able to learn in a variety of modes and more capable of unprecedented, experimental behavior. Dodge as we may, it looks like *we are it.* As our collective human consciousness is woven into an intelligent fabric, we are likely to find that we have been brought through this long journey to serve a purpose.

> **Gaia enters the stage of conscious evolu-**
> **tion by virtue of the development of her**
> **function of self-consciousness—Humanity.**

We need to know about this job—how to get there, how to carry it on, what to aspire to? By studying human evolution and the development of forms lower than the human, we can learn something about the principles and processes of evolution. However, it is impossible for us to observe *conscious evolution* in a direct way because we are just at the threshold of its time on this planet. And although other beings in the universe may have reached and even gone far beyond this stage, we humans have not yet developed the necessary capacities to study directly the higher levels of evolution.

We do, however, have one way to research what planetary conscious evolution might be. This is the study of unique individuals who have gone through the entire spectrum of evolutionary development: ontogeny recapitulates phylogeny. Studying the higher stages of individual transformation can perhaps help reveal a map that will guide us toward understanding planetary conscious evolution.

In the development of any evolutionary being there seem to be three stages: the preparatory stage of *personal harmonization,* or inner tuning; the stage of *transpersonal realization,* tuning to the whole; and the final stage of *conscious evolutionary service* or symphonic expression.

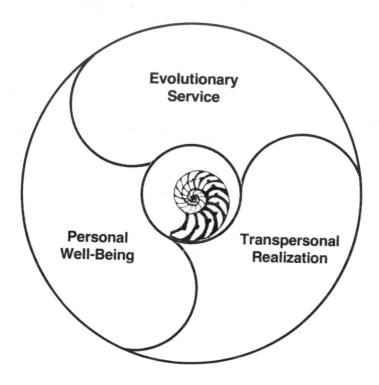

In the preparatory stage of *personal harmonization* the evolving being pays attention to self-development or self-perfection, and in time reaches a state of relative balance. This is like the tuning of an instrument. The strings of a violin, for example, are brought into harmonic relationship to one another. While this inner tuning clearly brings internal order, it can be accomplished in any key or even between keys and yet retain internal harmony. However, in order to play with others, the instrument is tuned to a standard or "true" key.

During the second stage of *transpersonal attunement* the being becomes conscious of itself as an integral part of its universe. This is the fine tuning of the violin to the orchestral whole. Again the tuning is to a true key that is known to create harmonious vibration in the psyche of the listener. The musician, the violin and the orchestra are now prepared for the next step.

In the third stage of *evolutionary service* there is volitional participation in the well-being and growth of the greater whole or universe. This is the period of artistic creativity or symphonic expression. This is the time of giving to the whole the best we have learned in the hope that we may serve. This is the stage in which the individual human, attuned to the consciousness of Humanity, enters into the great drama of planetary evolution.

Personal Harmonization

For a long time many of us have been experiencing a sense of incompletion. We have come to recognize that our conventional means of education, while preparing us for an interesting and prosperous life, modifies only the surface. There is no penetration. That which calls for transformation from deep within receives no response. Why is this? There is certainly no shortage of profound teachings that speak to the deepest in ourselves. How is it that we do not hear? What is it in us that obstructs this vital communication?

Something surrounding, something covering our sensitive inner self blocks the way—the personality. This lovable yet childish part of ourselves is full of fears and hiding, anger and demands, pain and blame. Here is where the work begins.

How to begin? What path shall we follow: ancient or modern, disciplined or free-form, ascetic or pleasurable? For the most part, traditional meditative paths focus immediately on transcendence of the physical and psychological aspects of the person. Yet it may be unwise to move too quickly. Before transcending the outer, conditioned personality, it may be prudent to put it in order, so that it will serve us well when we have found our life's work. Let us then look to paths that leave no stone unturned, that explore and align all facets of the person. In this way we have the possibility of attaining true personal and planetary integrity.

This understanding of the need for an integrated transformation of our physical, emotional, mental and spiritual selves is expressed in a number of modern teachings, most of which combine a traditional spiritual teaching with modern psychotherapeutic techniques.

Both Jung (1971) and Psychosynthesis (Assagioli, 1965) address in depth the personal and transpersonal aspects of life. Similarly, certain branches of Gurdjieff (Ouspensky, 1949), Yogic (Rama, 1976), and Sufi (Shah, 1977) paths seek the development of a harmoniously balanced person.

What are some of the steps by which this preparation is accomplished? The first step toward personal conscious evolution is *self-reflection*. The birth of a new quality of inner consciousness can be nurtured by the practice of self-observation. This is a gentle practice in which I seek the truth of myself, in which I seek to see without touching, without bringing preconceptions about how to be. In this practice of self-inquiry there is no attempt to change anything, except to deepen my capacity to see the situation, to see the laws of the universe at work in the inner world of the psyche. Though appearing to be a small thing, this is an immense step—the first turning inward.

Yet why not change, when so much is evidently wrong? It's the old story of the thousand-headed hydra: cut off one head here, and dozens of others appear. And these are perhaps even more destructive than the one that was eliminated. Symptom modification will not do the job; deep self-knowledge must precede change. Furthermore, that which we cut off may be only the negative expression of a profoundly valuable human quality. The suppression of anger is a well-known path to depression, while the acknowledgement and rechanneling of anger may provide a new source of strength and perseverance.

At some point, as self-knowledge deepens, a spontaneous harmonization, a gathering of the clan, begins to occur.

As the parts of myself are recognized as **aspects of one whole, conflicting and self-destructive behaviors start to diminish while constructive, integrative qualities ascend.**

This is the period of inner harmonization and the discovery of individual self. This harmonization, in contrast to earlier attempts to change, springs from a collaboration of the personality with a deep inner wisdom. Herein I begin a conscious work of accenting certain aspects of the personality and de-emphasizing others. In this gentle way those qualities which are most true to the self and to the work of conscious evolution are granted eminence.

Transpersonal Realization

An effective path of self-harmonization leads inevitably to the question of spirituality. As the consciousness behind personality becomes more and more awakened, the question of relationship to the context in which I exist begins impinging upon awareness. As the demand for attention by the ego diminishes, free energy becomes available for seeking deeper, transpersonal dimensions of consciousness. (Herein the "ego" is defined as that part of the personality which insists on seeing the self as separate from the rest of reality.) While the ego may have been quite essential in the earlier phases of personal integration, it now becomes less important. The energy formerly used to maintain the illusion of a separate self now becomes available for new, more inclusive modes of perception.

This stage is beyond the reconditioning of the personality. It is a quest for trans-conditioning, an exploration in consciousness. With a new-found sense of identity, the intention of becoming better is replaced by aspiration toward becoming more. Consciousness extends, as does light, in all directions—down into the depths of our subjective unconscious, up into the brilliance of our spiritual being. It encompasses more and more, inviting in dark shadowy creatures of fear and fury as well as angelic beings of light and love. There is no turning back; the journey has begun.

For support on this journey there are available at present a rich variety of approaches generally referred to as paths of meditation. Meditation, from the Latin *meditatio*, means "a thinking over," an overthought, a larger vision of the reality in which we exist. As the vista of consciousness opens, it opens to a field of subtle energies.

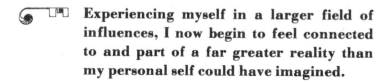 **Experiencing myself in a larger field of influences, I now begin to feel connected to and part of a far greater reality than my personal self could have imagined.**

At this stage, breakthroughs, peak experiences, entirely new sorts of understanding may flower into consciousness. I now begin to experience a complete revolution in orientation: I now come to see and understand myself in a living holistic universe.

This revolution, this new-born sense of participation in a greater reality is often confounding to my previous sense of self. A powerful urge to retreat is likely to arise at this point on the journey. Fortunately, however, at just this moment of darkness, help may be received from a higher level of consciousness than that which is making the attempt. With the reception and integration of this subtle yet compelling inspiration there is again a moment of connection and understanding. Henceforth, the lower, separative consciousness will listen and respond to this guidance as a means of support in the quest for transformation to a new level of being.

Conscious Evolutionary Service

As a result of the harmonization of personality (first stage), combined with a deep connection to sources of inner wisdom (second stage), the individual now discovers unique talents and abilities to contribute to the work of conscious evolution. This is the beginning of the path of service (third stage.)

The term service (as used herein) describes work that finds its source of inspiration and direction deep within the human psyche. Each of us has a particular role to play, a unique potential that I come to know as my consciousness deepens. This call comes from and expresses a deep understanding of unity. This is a form of love, a love that connects me with a larger reality—not the personal love of one being for another, but a transpersonal love for the greater Being of which we are all a part.

How can the phase of conscious evolution be understood in relation to the larger process of evolution?

> "Evolution" is the development of any type of energy organization or being which progresses to a more conscious and purposeful role in the Universe. "Conscious evolution" is that latter phase in evolutionary process wherein the developing entity becomes conscious of itself, aware of the process in which it is involved and begins voluntarily to participate in the work of evolution.

This can happen in a number of dimensions, in a number of ways, and in fact has been happening for a long while both in individuals and small groups. We are now approaching that moment in evolutionary history when Humanity as one self-conscious entity will assume this role.

In preparation for this unified function much work is required. And, in fact, many individuals and groups are working diligently. There is an *Aquarian Conspiracy* (Ferguson, 1980). Although each may express the aim quite differently (i.e. work for the common good, alleviation of suffering for all sentient beings, service to God, etc.), each activity that may be called conscious evolution shares the common goal of intentional service to something beyond our personal subjective needs.

What then are some types of service moving us forward toward a unified human work? All truly socially beneficial projects fall in this category. The Salvation Army, various welfare projects, hospitals, etc., all have the alleviation of human suffering in mind. This is the Bodhisattva path, the very basis of service.

The work of scientific enquiry and creativity also prepares us, for the task of conscious evolution by empowering us in our relationship with material reality. For example, advanced communication technology now permits us to send and receive information almost instantaneously from all parts of the planet. In this manner Gaia begins her development of a new nervous system. Similarly the work of ecologists indicates a growing planetary sensitivity. The exacting study of organic and inorganic ecosystems clearly demonstrates a tendency toward conscious evolutionary activity.

The current resurgence of interest in psychological and spiritual development indicates another major category of service. In every walk of life a growing dissatisfaction with our old ways of being has become evident. As a result there is an abundance of creative experimentation in the development of a "technology" of human transformation. This work very directly prepares us for a new age.

However, while these areas of service—good works, scientific enquiry and psychological development—clearly serve the emergence of planetary consciousness, those who do this work often do not see or acknowledge this function. On the other hand, the work that can truly be regarded as serving Gaia will be initiated consciously and choicefully. We are just today, in the latter decades of the Twentieth Century, beginning to understand our profound potential for conscious evolutionary service. Some lines of work that point in this direction include: discovering and projecting positive thought forms (Chapter 3); practicing methods of spiritual realization (Chapter 7); channeling guidance from higher transpersonal sources of wisdom (Chapter 8); and experimenting with the development and potentials of group consciousness (Chapter 10).

There are apparently other ways of practicing conscious evolution that are both beyond the scope of this book and beyond the reach of contemporary Humanity as we are today. One such way is the great work of transmitting powerful healing energies directly from the cosmos to the subtle bodies of Humanity and the planet. Sri Aurobindo, for example, is said to have devoted himself, both during and after his physical incarnation, to channeling the necessary energies for the birth of a new age.

One special way of serving conscious evolution (discussed in the following chapter), with which many are now experimenting, is through the discovery and expression of thought-forms that are attuned to and aligned with the greater evolutionary process. This is a subtle work, one that deserves a great deal of research. For it is not just by hearing a thought or by holding a thought, but by the way in which we relate to a thought that gives it the potency to transform reality. This book is an experiment in that direction, an attempt to offer a way of viewing reality that will lead us toward conscious evolution—upstream with the salmon.

Chapter 3

WE ARE WHAT WE THINK

"All that we are is the result of what we
have thought: it is founded on our thoughts, it
is made up of our thoughts. If a man speaks or
acts with a pure thought, happiness follows
him, like a shadow that never leaves him."
(Dhammapada)

The belief that *thought creates reality* has been with us a
long time. For many millenia individuals and groups have

31

secretly practiced, for better or worse, the art of this magic.
Using the power of thought, both the good guys and the bad
guys have tampered with and influenced the course of human
history. We, all of us alive today, have been profoundly influenced by this long-standing chess game.

There is little we can do about the past. But there is a great
deal we can do, both individually and collectively, about the
present and the future. However, before we can change the
outer forms of our life we must first change the inner forms—
the thoughts, beliefs and values which have created the world
we live in. For instance, almost without exception, each of us
sees ourself as a separate entity—a thing apart from the context
in which we live. We are taught this from early childhood and
therefore can barely imagine an alternative sense of personal
identity. Yet an abundance of evidence, drawn both from
intuitive or mystical insight and from scientific energy field
measurement, demonstrates the contrary—

**We simply do not exist except as parts of a
larger reality.**

How on earth have we, the Western culture, managed to
forget this? How is it that we have come so far and still do not
understand the basic fabric of the universe? How is it we do not
know the laws of manifestation and the ways in which our
inner and outer lives are conditioned? Somehow we of the West
have managed to turn things upside down. With much fanfare
we have created and defended a materialistic vision of how
things are—that which is most real is that which is most
tangible, visible and knowable by our sensory apparatus. From
this view, higher evolutionary forms such as the human being
have gradually and spontaneously emerged from the "basic
building blocks"—beginning of course with inanimate matter.
Life is a wonderful accident, and thought is considered an
artifact of the more fundamental reality of the material world.

By looking only in this one direction, we have cut ourselves off from the very fount of creation. In fact, the problematic external reality we are today experiencing is to a large degree the result of this one-sided mode of perception—we are what we think.

From the metaphysical perspective the opposite is true. The material universe—the objects and life forms we see around us —are viewed as a manifestation of divine thought, of that which already exists in subtler, non-physical realms of mind. Plato, in his work *The Republic* (1945), demonstrates how that which we call reality, that which is visible to our eyes (world of appearances) is but a dim shadow or reflection of the Ideal (intelligible world), that which is more perfect and true.

What seems to be necessary for those who take seriously our personal and planetary future, is an integrated understanding of both movements—of how, on the one hand, life spontaneously emerges from the primal ooze and how, on the other hand, life is called forth by divine intention.

For us, personally, this means studying how our lives emerge and develop in spite of our intentions. At the same time, this also means learning how we can and do create our lives by the thoughts, attitudes and beliefs we hold. We, both individually and as a species, are just beginning to realize that as we attain a clearer perception of how things work, we will better be able to co-create a future that reflects our deepest values.

An Idea Whose Time Has Come

The idea that apparent reality is both a reflection and a manifestation of higher reality seems to be an idea whose time has come—an idea that is ripe for inclusion in the general human psyche. We find ourselves at a point in evolutionary history where all of our potency and efficacy is called for. No longer can emotional inclination or rational technology be depended on to guide us through the current crisis. In order to bring forth a new reality we need now to include more subtle levels of understanding and creativity.

Fortunately we are not left to our own resources alone. In a magnificence of ways and forms, the idea of "thought power" springs forth, apparently of itself. All around us we see our friends practicing the manifestation of money, love, self-regard and even parking places. The time of manifestation is upon us. The challenge is to extract the essence of our learning from these many experiments and to practically direct this new-born understanding toward the greater work of conscious evolution.

How does all this work? Let us begin from the top. "In the beginning God (the highest) created the heavens (higher reality) and the earth (manifest reality)." So it is in all creation stories. First the Divinity, then Divine Thought, then the intention to create matter and life, and lastly, the manifestation. From this perspective all of manifest reality is the expression of divine thought.

Why does the Divinity bother to create such a plethora of magnificence and confusion? The accounts are numerous and varied. In one story God is bored up there in heaven all alone with no friends, no one to argue or play with. So, it is said, the Supreme Being created the angels. But they were so busy with the precise ordering of reality and with the harmonics of beautiful song that God found no solace in them—no spark, no resistance. So God created humankind, with all our foibles. End boredom!

An alternate story a bit more seriously suggests that God, noticing the effects of time and age, decided to create a self-perpetuating life support system. This system would not only result in a myriad of beautiful forms, but would also produce self-conscious beings who would choose to serve and maintain the Whole in a perfect state of balanced energy exchange.

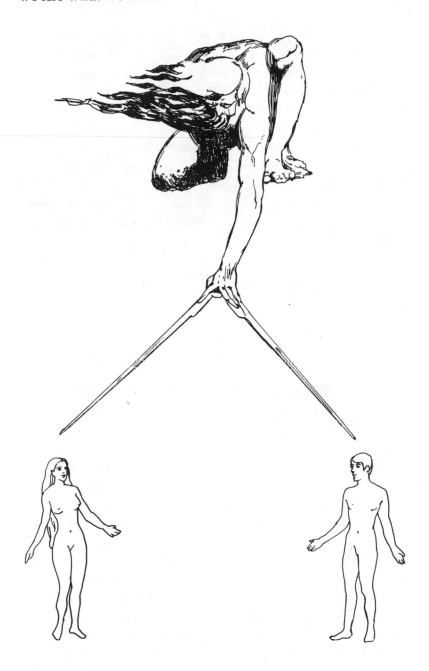

In this story, evolution is envisioned as conscious research. From somewhere on high the thought was formulated to initiate an experiment in developing beings capable of conscious evolutionary work. From a higher dimension our particular piece of work—the evolution of consciousness of planet Earth—may be simply one of many short-term projects. Yet to us the experiment appears an extremely long and difficult one. To us this experiment is of primary importance. In fact, it is a matter of life or death.

We are just now after billions of years figuring out the rules of the game, the possibilities of the adventure. Now that we perceive the game plan, how shall we learn to play?

Negative Perception

The quote at the beginning of this chapter suggests that:

> **All outer reality is born of thought, and we, either unconsciously or consciously, participate in the ongoing creation of the Universe.**

Whether or not we realize it, we do, to a large degree, create our physical and emotional reality by our thought processes, which in turn are based on our belief system. If we hold negative thoughts about ourselves or the world, we experience a negative life. As we hold judgmental, critical thoughts about others, we see and experience others through suspicion and fear. We are caught, in spite of our best intentions, in cultural thought patterns that we call our own, as if we had actually decided to be this way. We believe for example that competition fosters quality. Yet while this may be true for consumer commodities, the effects of this cultural belief on the individual psyche may be degenerative.

Yet we do know better. Each of us understands that something quite different is possible. Each of us knows that the
human condition is intrinsically noble.

Each of us intuitively realizes that we, our-
selves, as "children of God," are part of a
Universe that unfolds in response to an
intention greater than our own.

In spite of this intuitive vision, however, we see that we
defiantly hold onto and support an image of life that is fraught
with struggle and conflict.

The thought-form of perpetual struggle has dominated us for
longer than we care to remember. We see and experience
humankind in conflict with the environment, people harming
one another, nation against nation, man against woman and so
forth. This almost omnipresent perception of human experience as laden with misunderstanding, suffering and conflict is
created by our negative beliefs about reality. We see and
experience the results of this negativity all around us in bitter-
ness, crime, war and a pervasive sense of hopelessness.

From whence comes this difficulty? Are these self-defeating
perceptions that we so dearly cling to an accurate mirror of
reality, or are they perhaps ghosts of a long-forgotten past?
Brain theorist Richard Hodges of the Berkeley Brain Center (in
personal dialogue) offers an evolutionary explanation. The
human being possesses three brains, or centers of intelligence,
that have evolved over billions of years. During our early
mammalian period some two billion years ago, when our form
was much like the modern field mouse, life was very dangerous
for us. To survive and to find our sustenance it was necessary
to hide out in dark corners during the day and to creep out
with great caution in the depths of night. According to Hodges
this was the period of development of the second brain that
interacts with the environment by the establishment of
emotional response mechanisms. Surely a generalized fear

response was appropriate way back then, when we were so
young and vulnerable.

Each of us can still recognize this little fellow in our feelings
of sensitivity and vulnerability. Often we find ourselves fear-
fully alerted by something as innocent as the shadow of a bird
or the rustling of leaves in the wind.

Today, however, environmental survival is no longer the
issue. Yet we are still animated by an ancient perceptual
modality—one that conjures up malignant phantoms at each
unrecognized sound, one that retreats into the darkness at the
appearance of other living forms. We have physically evolved
far beyond this stage, we have even grown another brain, yet
psychologically we are often dominated by these ancient tendencies. In a time when courage is called for, fearful negative
imagery still unconsciously controls much of our life.

Mass media brilliantly exemplifies our negative perceptual
mode, and ironically creates it anew every day with countless
stories of violence and injustice. The front page of a local
newspaper recently reported two armed conflicts, a murder, a
tax evasion scandal and the exposure of political torture
chambers. This extremely grim picture of the day's events is
obviously the result of *a careful selection* from thousands of
bits of information. Why do we continue to prime ourselves

with the most negative perceptions available? Surely something quite different is needed. For instance, why not publish a major periodical entitled "The Good News?" The headlines could announce—in bold type—important scientific break-throughs, profound spiritual experiences, and socially benefi-cial projects. Who knows what the impact might be?

These stories and illustrations demonstrate how we allow ourselves and our reality to be dominated by unconscious negative thought-forms.

Clearly the time is ripe to awaken and to begin to generate positive evolutionary thoughts that enliven and enlighten our reality.

Restructuring Perceptual Reality

Perhaps all of this darkness has been necessary. Perhaps the perception of ourselves competing for survival has served an important function in allowing us to differentiate as indi-viduals, as groups, and as a species. Perhaps it has been necessary for us as individuals to separate from our parents. Perhaps it has been important for us as a species to separate from the mass consciousness of the animal kingdom. Perhaps it has been required that we sort ourselves out and differentiate from the all-encompassing intelligence of the universe in order to learn the skills of co-creatorship.

However, the relevance of separative consciousness has now run its course. We are now ready to integrate the discriminative and the intuitive modes of perception. This is the unity of the West and East spoken of so often. This is the integration of the left and right brains. This is the experience of wholeness that we all so deeply long for.

We awaken to ourselves midway in the evolution of planetary consciousness. This is the age of conscious choice. This is the age in which Gaia discovers self-consciousness. This is the age in which her child—Humanity as a self-conscious being—is born.

Rather than seeing outer reality as something to grapple with, we can now choose our dominant modes of thought and perception and thereby influence the reality we experience.

The possibility of altering our reality by carefully choosing our thought patterns now comes into view. We can begin with the practice of shifting our perceptions, beliefs and values in such a way that our deeper aims may be actualized. Yet we can only make this change by first choosing to believe in ourselves. It has been said in days of old that:

Faith is necessary—faith that thoughts do create reality, faith that we as individuals can change our mode of perception and the quality of our experience, and faith that we, collectively, can influence the process of human and planetary evolution.

Over and over we have been told that something wonderful is possible. If we wish to be free from our self-created prison we must courageously begin the task. First we *recognize* and then *let go* of our preconditioned beliefs, thoughts and behaviors. As I believe people are basically dangerous, I create danger; as I believe they are inherently loving, I create love.

Our beliefs have been given to us without our consent. They do not actually belong to us. And since many of them are not working very well, we may as well give them back and opt for new ones that are intended to fulfill our needs and potentials. It is just that simple. And yet this can only be done as an act of will—as a voluntary choice to go against the tide of our pre-determined reaction patterns.

> In speaking of evolution it is necessary to understand from the outset that no mechanical evolution is possible. Human evolution is the evolution of will, and 'will' cannot evolve involuntarily. Human evolution is the evolution of the power of doing, and 'doing' cannot be the result of things which 'happen.'
>
> (Ouspensky, 1949:58)

How shall we prepare ourselves for this wonderful task of conscious evolution? We begin with the work of individual awakening, first to self-consciousness and then to a larger reality. This work implies the painfully honest practice of self-examination wherein our attitudes, beliefs and perceptions come to be recognized as products of the mind, rather than aspects of objective reality. Once this is seen, serious self-inquiry can commence.

What do we see as we look inward? What are the mechanics of the individual psyche? Careful self-observation discloses subtle relationships between the physical, emotional and mental processes. Impressions from the outside world stimulate sensory responses that trigger pre-conditioned emotional reactions. These in turn activate pre-determined unconscious thought patterns. For example, a form appears that is recognized as a four-legged creature (already a good bit of interpretation has occurred). One person sees a loving, overgrown puppy. Feelings of warmth and caring are generated within and emanate into the environment, influencing the animal's behavior toward friendliness. The original image of "gentle dog" is reinforced. On the other hand. . .a negative thought can easily attract a nasty bite on the leg. In this way, existing beliefs about reality are continually corroborated and strengthened. Well fortified, these unconscious, mechanical thought-forms continue to reign and determine all subsequent perception and experience. This is true for us personally and globally.

This view of manifestation is the very opposite of what we have been taught to understand. We have been told that ideas are based on experience. We now see that experience itself can be a consequence of thought, and that thoughts can result from our conscious intentions to mold reality.

There are, however, a few obstacles in our path. One of the major difficulties to which we humans are particularly prone is our identification with (or belief in) the mind's interpretations of the messages sent by turbulent emotions. Thus, calming the sea of emotional/mental activity is a prerequisite of conscious work.

Toward this end it is necessary first to recognize the identifications and projections as wonderful fantasies, and then to consciously separate the automatic thought patterns from the initial emotional responses. An anxiety arises in relation to a financial problem. The problem cannot be clearly addressed and resolved because of the anxiety. The anxiety in turn cannot be calmed down because of the problem. This is truly a vicious circle—an unholy alliance of mutual support. How to work with this dilemma?

A surgical stroke is necessary to separate the parts. The anxiety must be isolated and sensed directly while the problem must be recognized as a process of mental association. Within the psyche the two can be separated and held apart. Only after this separation has been made is it possible to apply effectively relaxation techniques toward calming the sea of emotional storm.

For example, a friend tells the following story. Once while traveling in Afghanistan through the Hindu Kush mountains the fuel pump of the hired car exploded and left him and his son stranded in a high mountain pass. The more he thought about how poorly constructed the car was, the more distressed he became. However, in a flash, something in himself recognized the opportunity and decided to alter the automatic sequence of inner events. He first recognized a sharp contrast between his expectation of the day and how it was actually unfolding. This had resulted in an experience of anger, which in turn was expressed in a stream of negative judgments toward the car and destiny in general. Upon this recognition he was able to separate the irritation and the event, and to redirect his attention toward the remarkably beautiful environment in which he found himself. Soon his irritation was replaced by a sense of gratitude and heightened perception. It has been said, even these days, that the practice of such transformation can result, in time, in a complete shift of one's spontaneous mode of perception.

Along with this sorting and calming of the emotional/thought processes, a gradual balancing and harmonization of the physical, emotional and mental energies may be activated, along with a new sense of personal well-being. One is no longer dominated by the head, the emotions, or sexual drives. In addition, one's awareness becomes free to include more, to embrace that which is too subtle and gentle to compete with the egoistic demands, that which waits patiently for recognition. A subtle yet deep sense of self is born.

Also, as a deeper sense of self is realized, a contact with *conscience* becomes active. Gurdjieff (Ouspensky, 1949) speaks about objective conscience, a direct perception of that which is true and necessary. As conscience becomes awakened, the individual begins, both from self-interest and interest in the whole, to wish to serve, to give something toward the transformation of human and planetary experience. In this way, little by little, we are drawn into right relationship with Gaia.

If we, Humanity, continue to produce malignant energies, the planet soon will respond, as would any healthy organism;

disruptive elements are either absorbed, rejected or re-formed. It looks like it's up to us to re-form ourselves and to reintegrate with Mother-Earth in the symphony of a new age.

Evolutionary Guidance

For each person it is necessary to find the unique central purpose of his or her life, to find the higher thought that is attempting to express itself in and through the mind and life and activity of that person.

In some cases the individual experiences a direct communication—words or symbols—of such intensity that there is an
immediate shift in perception and life direction. Outer and
inner worlds become imbued with deep meaning and everyday
behavior is summoned into alignment with the new-found
purpose. Such was the experience of Alfred Watkins, (Michell,
1969) who is known to have introduced the idea of ley lines—
currents of subtle energy that are said to flow along the Earth's
surface. One day in 1921 Watkins sat on a hill overlooking the
countryside. While enjoying the beauty of the scene, he also gazed
at a map of the area. All of a sudden, much to his amazement,
the map began to transform itself. In a flash of inspiration, he
saw a web of connecting lines, relating hilltops, churches, mounds
and ancient temples. He saw in his mind's eye the ancient
system of ley lines. Henceforth his life was directed by his own
need to understand his vision more clearly and to share this
new understanding with the world.

For others the discovery of purpose comes gradually. The
realization of what one wants or is called to do creeps up, as it
were, little by little. One simply "finds oneself" assuming a
task, just because it seems important.

As the central purpose of one's life becomes clear, there is
often a realization that what we wish for is identical with what
we are asked to give. There is perfect alignment here between
what is good for the individual and what is good for the whole.
For example, an individual's urge toward a new scientific
understanding may add to the common knowledge. A person's
need for self-expression through music may bring just the right
tone to the orchestration of Humanity.

As the specific purpose clarifies itself, the higher thought
that the purpose expresses also becomes more and more clear.
This can then be placed in juxtaposition to the beliefs and
thoughts that are currently dominating the individual's life. A
work of transformation is then taken on. The challenge is to
allow unconscious, dominating thought-forms to recede from

power, and to bring forward through *intention* consciously chosen evolutionary thought.

For example, when working as part of a group or organization, internal conflicts may be perceived as the result of power struggle, egoistic selfishness or even plain stupidity. Each of these negative evaluations perpetuates the conflict and even steers it in the direction of that particular perception. On the other hand, one can choose to view the situation differently. This choice may be to regard what is occurring as an evolutionary process involving the identification of unique talents and the specialization of functions. Intentionally holding such a perspective will without doubt influence and transform the situation.

At this point the individual begins to practice co-creation. For this work it is not only necessary to know the higher thought or purpose that one serves. It also becomes essential to know the aim, the specific way in which the purpose needs to be expressed. In this way the pure intention or thought that is entering worldly manifestation moves from the abstract to the concrete. There is magic in this, to be sure.

> It is the aim of that branch of esoteric science which is popularly called Magic, to obtain control of conditions upon one plane by acting upon the forces of the plane immediately above it, which acts as causal plane to the lower one. White Magic is distinguished as that exploitation of knowledge which aims at harmonizing and uplifting existence along the lines of advancing evolution, and which, though it may concentrate its effort upon a particular point, excludes from its benefits nothing which by its nature is capable of receiving them."
>
> (Fortune, 1974:14)

It is important, even essential, to begin the practice of this magic. While subtle skills can only be learned by inner experimentation, basic steps can be outlined:

- I recognize my negative thoughts, beliefs and attitudes.
- I choose to see these as phantom images and I agree to replace them.
- I select evolutionary principles and transformative thoughts and beliefs with which I feel in alignment.
- As an inner practice, I replace the former with the latter; I replace the dis-ease with the healthy, constructive and joyful images.

The work which is done individually can without question play a significant role in human and planetary evolution.

However, more and more we are receiving guidance that individual efforts are not nearly as effective as group work. It has been suggested that only the unified energies of a group of highly evolved individuals will permit the reception and transmission of the highly potent cosmic energies that are necessary and available to us. It seems likely that the development of group consciousness represents the next quantum leap in human evolution. This step can lead toward the harmonization and awakening of the unified consciousness of Humanity.

In summary: rather than seeing our outer reality as something to grapple with, we can now choose our dominant modes of thought and perception, and thereby influence the reality we experience.

In order to make this transition it is helpful to study principles and processes by which a conscious evolution might be realized. The following chapters introduce some positive thoughts in this direction—toward a positive future, now.

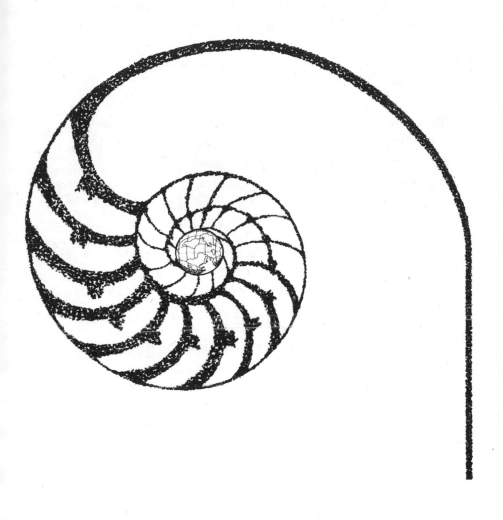

An Opening

Ten basic principles and processes of evolutionary transformation have been woven into a tapestry that summarizes the challenge of conscious evolution. These principles are clearly visible in our everyday lives—within our individual selves, within the groupings we form, within humanity as a potentially integrated organism, and within the living being of Gaia, the planet Earth.

All ten principles describe basic life processes from an evolutionary perspective. They make explicit the assumption that everything is inspired by an *inner intention* toward greater order, increased complexity and higher, participative consciousness.

By choosing to hold these or similar principles in mind and by choosing to *align* our lives with them, we enter the process of conscious evolution.

The list is partial, intended to be summary for the sake of clarity. Nonetheless, taken together they form a coherent picture of the operative patterns of evolutionary change. One principle out of context makes only partial sense. Only in relationship to one another does the meaning emerge.

How can they be helpful? As expressions of the unitive evolutionary pattern they can serve as templates for our thought. As we align our subjective thought patterns with evolutionary principles, an inner attunement can occur. They can serve as a reference, a way in which we can confirm our observations of reality. They are tuning forks that allow our subjective mind to attune to the larger intelligence of the Universe.

PART II

PRINCIPLES OF CONSCIOUS EVOLUTION

Chapter 4: **Cosmic Glue: Three Metaprinciples**
Unity; Perpetual Transcendence; and
Correspondence. Within the context of
total unity, the multi-dimensional Universe
calls forth perfect harmony and joyful
transcendence.

Chapter 5: **Becoming Self: Principles of
Development**
Differentiation; Integration; and Nucleation. As the parts identify their unique
roles, a central guiding intelligence
emerges that will care for the integrity
and transformation of the whole.

Chapter 6: **The Fabric of Love:
Principles of Relationship**

Synergy; Attunement; Alignment; and
Quantum Transformation. As an evolving
being attunes to and aligns with the intention of universal evolution, creative energy
is spontaneously available for radical
transformation.

Chapter 4
COSMIC GLUE

Three Metaprinciples

Since principles already describe basic universal processes, what *on Earth* are metaprinciples? Are they necessary?

Metaprinciples have a special function. They go beyond describing a recurrent life pattern or theme. They embrace and call attention to the fundamental underlying interdependence of all being. Even though they can be described in words, they are of such essential profundity that they also call

for an entirely different mode of understanding. They ask that
we open our hearts, minds and spirits to a direct perception of
universal integrity.

Unity, the overarching principle that embraces all others,
describes the essential interdependent relationship of all that
is. *Perpetual Transcendence* describes the perfect balance of
universal energy exchange. *Correspondence* describes the
analogous operation of basic laws and patterns on multiple
levels of being.

Unity

 **Everything at every moment exists in
living, interdependent relationship.
Nothing is separate. Everything influences
everything else. All is one.** *

Traditional mystical schools throughout the ages have
described the highest experience as one of knowing directly the
fundamental unity of all being. Realization of the ultimate
unity is the highest aim, the 'summum bonum' of inner paths
of spiritual development.

> In esoteric or Kabbalistic tradition, this dualism
> (servant and Lord) is overcome by a
> monotheism which reaches its final conclusion,
> its real and infinite significance, where God is
> one, not only in his Lordship but in his whole

---

*Descriptions of principles are by the author.

> reality; he is the one in the absolute sense, the
> 'One without a second,' the only reality so that
> everything which exists is in essence God.
> (Schaya, 1973:137)

All traditional religious paths are designed to lead Humanity, individually and collectively, to this fundamental understanding. However, during the last two hundred years, the Western World has gone through a "fall," a forgetfulness, a misunderstanding of separative thought from which we are just now re-emerging. Surprisingly, it is science itself (often blamed for our demise) that seems to be spearheading the breakthrough. Einstein's work in the beginning of this century, which shattered the foundations of Newtonian physics, opened the way and even made necessary a new, less linear model of the Universe. We are still searching for this model. Hopefully, it will be more integrative and more joyful.

In 1969, Lawrence LeShan published a fascinating article in which he presented 62 statements descriptive of some phase of reality. With the exception of a few key words, it was almost impossible to distinguish those statements made by traditional mystics from those made by contemporary scientific theorists. Fritjof Captra's book, *The Tao of Physics*, insightfully demonstrates how the modern scientific conception of the universe is merging with the ancient truths.

> The basic oneness of the universe is not only
> the central characteristic of the mystical experi
> ence, but is also one of the most important
> revelations of modern physics. It becomes
> apparent at the atomic level and manifests
> itself more and more as one penetrates deeper
> into matter, down into the realm of subatomic
> particles. The unity of all things and events
> will be a recurring theme throughout our com-

parison of modern physics and Eastern
philosophy.

(1975:131)

Similarly, in the last ten years, the field of holography has
appeared to reassert the fundamental unity of the universe.
Holography, however, goes even further: in addition to every
separate thing being related to everything else, it looks as if
every separate thing may contain a photograph-like image of
the entire universe. Not only is everything related to every other
thing, but everything *is* everything. We begin to see as we try to
grasp these ideas, that our Western rational intellect, from
which we usually attempt to understand reality is inadequate.
We are coming to a period of synthesis, a time when rational
thought is being called into intimate relationship with holistic
vision.

Further, not only is there one unity, but there are unities
within unities within unities, etc. Within the Universe, from an
astronomical, macrocosmic perspective, we see the Galaxy as a
unity reflecting all the laws that are operative in the greater
Universe. Within the Galaxy, we see the Solar System as a unity
reflecting the same laws. Within the Solar System, Planet
Earth is a unity, and so on.

We are not alone, we are without question intimately wed to
all of creation.

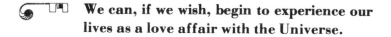 **We can, if we wish, begin to experience our
lives as a love affair with the Universe.**

Beginning from a microcosmic perspective, there are wave-
particles within atoms, atoms within molecules, molecules
within cells, cells within organs, organs within individual
beings, individual beings within planetary entities, planetary
entities within solar beings, solar beings within galactic angels,
galactic angels within unknown realms of consciousness,

unknown realms of consciousness within universes, universes within the All.

Within the unity of Gaia we see that each individual, each cell in the planetary being, is interrelated with every other cell.

Every action, feeling, thought and intuitive insight has a small but definite influence on everything else on the planet. There is no separation. We are part of one being.

The principle of Unity hides only from those who actively deny it. It is immediately available to us. To the degree that we hold the principle of Unity in mind, we begin to notice subtle connecting webs of energy. We begin to see and feel directly the implicit unity of all being.

Perpetual Transcendence

🐚 ⌨ **Within unity, there is a coherent system of balanced energy exchange that offers the opportunity for continual transformation into the unknown.**

Humankind has long known of the perfect balance of energies within the universe. However, we of the Western World have forgotten again, fallen into "ignorance." That is, we have ignored what we already know. During the last century we have somehow managed to come up with the principle of entropy. As a result, a great fear has crept into our being. Is the Universe disintegrating, moving farther and farther away from itself into boundless space and ultimate separation? All of our fears of loneliness and isolation are triggered by this notion of entropy as a dominant principle.

Just in time, however, we have rediscovered the principle of Syntropy. Arising from both the scientific and metaphysical domains, syntropy appeases our fears of Divine indifference and rekindles our hope for the future. Buckminster Fuller comes to the heart of the matter:

> The history of man seems to demonstrate the emergence of his progressively conscious participation in theretofore spontaneous universal evolution. . .My continuing philosophy is predicated. . .on the assumption that in dynamic counterbalance to the expanding universe of entropically increasing random disorderliness there must be a universal pattern of omnicontracting, convergent, progressive orderliness and that man is the anti-entropic reordering function. . .   (1963:xii)

Similarly, Szent-Gyorgyi (1974), in his observation of the drive in living matter to perfect itself, also talks about the *syntropic* process, this process by which the Universe reconstitutes itself:

> But there is mounting evidence for the existence of the opposite principle: syntropy—or 'negative entropy'—through the influence of which forms tend to reach higher and higher levels of organization, order and dynamic harmony.
>
> (1974:12)

From the metaphysical perspective, in the Yogic tradition, syntropy is known as the "in-breath" of Brahma. Seen in relation to the exhalation of manifestation, the vision of a perfectly balanced Universe appears. In Ouspensky's work, *In Search of the Miraculous* (1949), G. Gurdjieff describes the relationship of involuntionary (entropy) and evolutionary (syntropy) transformational processes. Together, they comprise the "reciprocal maintenance of the universe."

How does this work? The involutionary process refers to a decrease in rate of vibration from the highest to the lowest—down into dense, concrete matter or out into random, disorganized chaos. Fundamentally, this movement constitutes a decrease in consciousness. Evolution or syntropy, however, is the converse, a complementary process whereby matter is reclaimed, revivified and redirected toward the Source. This is the upswing of the circle, the return of the serpent's tale that feeds into the mouth to be recycled again and again.

In order to participate consciously in the **syntropic evolutionary process, beings must reach a certain level of development wherein they choose to devote their energy to a larger service.**

The work, then, is to gather together, or concentrate, random or chaotic bits of energy and to bring forth meaning, coherence and integration. This can be done on the physical, emotional, mental or higher spiritual planes. In each case, we have a calling together of disparate, relatively unrelated energies into more highly organized patterns, imbued with increased consciousness. This process can be seen in development of an embryo, in the evolution of the human species and in the infant art of computerized intelligence. All this unfolds as a great universal dance, a simultaneous exchange of energies. Involutionary transformations flow down through the realms of consciousness into concrete manifestation, while restorative evolutionary processes refine and return the energy to its source.

Gurdjieff notes that this is a possible work for the individual in any moment: through the concentration of energy or attention within the self, a higher quality of life comes into being for the moment and contributes to the larger evolutionary work. He calls this process *self-remembering*, a calling back of the lost members of the self, a reconstitution of that which eternally is.

Identification of true evolutionary processes constitutes an important area of research. What human capacities shall we develop? What lines of technology will best serve our evolutionary development? These questions must be addressed if we are to contribute to universal harmony. It is just such inquiry and participation that has been called by ancient tradition the Great Work.

While all this balancing of energies is keeping the Universe lovingly held together, there is another, perhaps even more challenging, process in motion. This is transcendence into the unknown. This is the joyful adventure of evolution.*

---

*See Appendix B for further discussion.

It is most likely that the human being in our current earthly form has never and will never appear again in the Universe. We are unique—an unprecedented event in evolutionary history. The life, the world, the being that we now choose to become (as we explore conscious evolution) will be another unique event.

> **There are no clear-cut guidelines, no** **rules, only potentials. The results of our exploration and works on the planet will be the test of our capacity for conscious evolutionary service.**

Correspondence

> **The same laws and principles operate** **analogously on all levels of manifestation.**

> True without any error; certain, very true; That which is Above, is as that which is below; and that which is below, is as That which is Above; for achieving the Wonders of the Universe. . .

This is the basic principle from *The Emerald Tablet* of Hermes Trismigistus: "As Above, so below"—fundamental laws, principles and processes of relationship manifesting analogously in a number of different dimensions. Electrons spin *in relation to* a central nucleus; groups of people gather *in relation to* a leader or vision; planets revolve *in relation to* a sun. This is the idea of macro-cosmos and micro-cosmos; tiny cosmoses within larger cosmoses within even larger cosmoses within the absolute cosmos—each acted upon by the same forces.

The *Kybalion* states it thusly:

> This principle embodies the truth that there is
> always a correspondence between the laws and
> phenomena of the various planes of Being and
> Life.
>
> (Three Initiates, 1908:27)

Again, this knowledge reaches us from antiquity. And again, we have forgotten. As separative consciousness has come to dominate our perception, we have come to see reality on one level only.

Gradually, the idea of a multi-dimensional reality has receded from our awareness, leaving us with a sense of flatness. We feel now a need to know again that there is much more to this world than meets the eye. We feel a need to remember that:

Our ordinary perception binds us to one **cosmos, while all the while a multidimensional Universe manifests in splendor before, yet invisible to, our very eyes.**

Fortunately, we are reawakening to the principle of Correspondence.

Lewis Thomas, in his book, *The Lives of a Cell*, takes the point of view that the planet itself can be seen as a cell:

> I have been trying to think of the earth as a
> kind of organism, but it is no go. I cannot
> think of it this way. It is too big, too complex,
> with too many working parts lacking visible
> connections. The other night, driving through a
> hilly, wooded part of southern New England, I
> wondered about this. If not like an organism,
> what is it like, what is it *most* like? Then, satis-

factorily for that moment, it came to me: it is *most* like a single cell.   (1975:4)

From the academic community, James Grier Miller's classic work, *Living Systems*, addresses the topic of correspondence through the laws of system theory.

The general living systems theory which this book presents is a conceptual system concerned primarily with concrete systems which exist in space-time. Complex structures which carry out living processes I believe can be identified at seven hierarchical levels—cell, organ, organism, group, organization, society, and supernatural system. My central thesis is that systems at all these levels are open systems which process inputs, throughputs, and outputs of various forms of matter, energy and information. . .Systems at each of the seven levels, I maintain, have the same 19 critical subsystems.   (1978:1)

Certainly we are once again getting the idea.

One night, a friend told a story: he had been watching a TV program about galaxies and noted that certain basic shapes reoccurred—spherical, spiral, elongated, etc. With this he was quite impressed. The following night, the same channel (coincidentally, as far as he knew) offered a program about micro-biological life in a swamp. Ecologists were researching the basic life support systems of the swamp, trying to identify the tiniest units in the chain of life. In describing their work, they noted that the organisms also took four or five basic shapes, which he noted, were almost identical to the galactic forms he had seen the night before.

The principle of Correspondence allows us to study general patterns of evolution through insights available to us on one level only, and thereby to apply our findings by analogy to other levels. From knowledge of cellular change we can formulate hypotheses about the transformation of individual or group consciousness. We can study individual growth and develop hypotheses about the transformation of planetary consciousness. And conversely we can study the planet and its movement in the solar system and understand by analogy processes that take place on the atomic level.

This emphasis on correspondence is not meant to diminish the uniqueness of the expression of these principles on each dimension. Each expression is special, different and worthy of research in and of itself. However, for the present discussion, the aim is to focus on that which relates apparently distinct evolutionary processes, rather than on that which differentiates them.

The term correspondence means "to be in conformity or agreement." To be in agreement with our evolutionary heritage is certainly the issue at hand.

The three principles of *Unity, Perpetual Life* and *Correspondence* offer a picture of the connective fabric—in space, time and eternity—of the living universe in which we find our being and purpose.

Chapter 5

Becoming Self

Principles of Development

From numerous possibilities, three developmental principles come into the foreground as especially relevant to evolution: Differentiation, Integration and Nucleation. Each plays a major role in the formation and transformation of evolutionary entities. Each is an expression of the ancient, deep, omnipresent wisdom of the cosmos. These are not our creation, but rather our instructions. From these we can begin to learn the mechanics of creation and thereby develop the understanding and skill necessary for co-creatorship.

Differentiation describes the development of separate parts, establishing unique identities, preparing for specialized functions. *Integration* describes the coordinated harmonious interrelationship of the parts in the service to the whole. *Nucleation* describes the emergence of a conscious center that holds responsibility for internal regulation and self-transcendence.

Differentiation

In each evolving being, the parts that are called to play specific, highly specialized roles differentiate to become unique and distinct from one another.

All organisms, from the atom with its submicroscopic wave/particles to the universe with its macrocosmic galactic worlds, have specialized sub-functions that perform vitally important tasks. In some instances, the parts develop their uniqueness before joining the organism; in other cases, specialized roles are developed during or after the formation of the organism. For example, in the eukaryotic cell mentioned earlier, it seems that the parts were highly differentiated, separate entities before their symbiotic union in the larger organism. At the same time, their specific function in relation to the cell fully emerged only after long evolutionary experimentation.

Other excellent examples of differentiated function within the context of the whole are found in the human organism. The organs—kidney, liver, heart, etc.—and the complex functions—digestive, respiratory, and nervous systems—only exist and have meaning in relation to the body as a unit. Unique differentiated parts, with specific functions, all work in harmony for the good of the whole. These parts and their specialized functions seem to have developed during the human evolution, rather than before.

In the Psychosynthesis model of individual growth (see Chapter 7), various parts of the personality—sub-personalities —are identified as quite distinct, functioning in almost complete isolation from one another. These separate sub-personalities may even be in conflict with one another. It may well be that in this initial isolation are found the very conditions necessary for the development of differentiated psychological functions.

Another example of the need for Differentiation is found in groups of individuals who gather together to serve a common aim. Often in the beginning the common aim is less potent than the need for self-differentiation of individual members. Hence, many such groups dissolve before the aim is accomplished. The difficulty here may have been that the group was formed prematurely, or that insufficient attention was given to the development of the unique individuality of each member before adherence to the common aim was called for.

While most functions serve the process of internal harmonization (health or homeostasis,) there is also another equally important group of functions that serve to stimulate transformation. These tendencies have no interest in how things have been; they are interested in change. Those parts of the individual that serve this function have been called 'evolutionary transformative agents' (ETA) or imaginal cells (Hubbard, 1978). They work to upset the status quo, to urge the evolving being toward potential self-transcendence.

In every organism there seem to be two different lines of development. One serves the involutionary movement of the Uni-

verse, the homeostatic/entropic function, while the other serves the evolutionary movement, the transformative/syntropic function. Both are necessary; both are good.

The homeostatic function maintains integrity and therefore lends force to stabilizing the organism at its current evolutionary stage. Conversely, the evolutionary functions lend their force to the transcendence of current life forms. Rohit Mehta (1961) refers to mutations as an expression of this tendency. One unruly member of a species chooses to change its form and thereby influences the development of the entire species. This mutant organism is often seen by other members of the group as ill-adapted, inadequate and certainly inappropriate to the current values of the culture. Nonetheless, it is just this strange, maladapted creature that is likely to take the leap into the unknown evolutionary future. Each mutant is an apparent outcast, a highly differentiated member of its species, going against the current, so to speak. Some make it, some don't.

How then does this principle relate to the larger vision of conscious evolution? Especially for humankind, the principle of Differentiation highlights the vital importance of allowing, valuing and even nurturing difference. Rather than attempting to subdue individual and cultural uniqueness, to homogenize Humanity, we wish to accent differences in human type. We wish to acknowledge the non-conformist as a potential agent of evolution.

 Respect for Differentiation can lead us to a deeper understanding of evolutionary process and can allow us to support specialized individuals and groups who explore and develop the mutant conscious-

ness necessary for the leap into an age of **conscious evolution.**

Integration

In each evolutionary being there is a unification and harmonization of the parts in service of the health and transformation of the whole.

This remarkable principle brings meaning to the process of Differentiation. The principle of Integration reflects the larger metaprinciple of Unity. Integration describes the action of a universal force that penetrates and draws together all of creation into one harmonious pattern.

We see this on every level of manifestation. We see it clearly in the formation of the eukaryotic cell. Strange bedfellows, these distinct symbiants coming together to form a single entity, coming together to prepare the way for subsequent modalities of earthly evolution. We see Integration remarkably exemplified in the human body, with its organs and systems interpenetrating and interrelating in one thriving life system. We see Integration in the functioning of highly developed groups, serving a common purpose on a level beyond the possibilities of individuals working separately. And we now see the potential for the Integration of the human species, for the evolution of the planetary Human Being.

During the process of Differentiation, membranes around the differentiated parts are formed whereby each part isolates itself from the surrounding environment to allow for unobstructed internal growth. During Integration, these separative membranes are transformed into filters. Thus an exchange of energy flowing through the membranes becomes possible as the part assumes its role in the function of the whole. This exemplifies the unifying principle of the Universe, the internal factor in evolution, the calling into service. In a word, this is the principle of love.

This love, however, is not simply the love of one part for another; it is also the love of each part for a higher evolutionary purpose. So in all cases where there is true Integration, there is also a calling to something higher, something of inherently great value to which the part can direct its love.

Integration primarily serves the stabilization and harmonization of the organism. It calls together the parts on each level of organization, whether that be cell, body, group, Humanity or planet. This process works in us, around us, and through us. It is omnipresent and omniscient. It is God's love. Since the influence of Integration is operative at all times, both visibly and invisibly, much can be gained from researching the action of this principle. As our observations progress, we are likely to note in every formative process the presence of an intentionality far greater than our own.

Nucleation

  In each evolving being a center is formed, a center that has in mind the integrity of the organism itself, the establishment of

right relationship with the environment, and the transcendent evolution of the organism.

The center, or nucleus, embodies in itself the integral pattern of the whole, the DNA, the picture of the organism in its perfect form. The nucleus also embodies the RNA, the messenger unit by which the nucleus will communicate the knowledge of its form to subsequent generations.

Further, the nucleus contains a third, hitherto unrecognized potential—the ETA, the evolutionary transformative agent. This rascal intelligence is constantly on the lookout for a means of upsetting the applecart, for a chance to change the way things are, just to see what will happen. Without the ETA, evolution would not be. This is the quality that instinctively understands the greater plan and willingly tries, in every possible way, to move a bit in that direction. As a result of the secretive work of the ETA, cells split into two, little life forms join together, strange mutant creatures are born, and all manner of unusual beings come into existence. The ETA serves as the transcendent function of the nucleus.

The nucleus, then, is the central intelligence of the organism. It permits Differentiation and calls for Integration. It fosters communication between the parts, balances their relationships, and controls and transforms processes that are out of synch. The nucleus initiates healing and even consoles the parts when they are upset. Even within the nucleus there seems to be a center—the nucleus of the nucleus, the center of the center. At the center is Divine mystery, invisible intelligence.

The principle of Nucleation is apparent in the structure of the atom, evident in our vision of the cell. We see Nucleation in the group that gathers around a central leader or a unifying purpose. We see the principle danced out with great beauty in the Sufi ceremony of the whirling dervishes. Herein the sheik, who is also called the center or pole, swirls clockwise in the

center, while the murids or students whirl around the outside in
reverse direction. This revolution around a nuclear center,
reflecting the movement of the solar system, causes us to
wonder upon the wisdom of the sun.

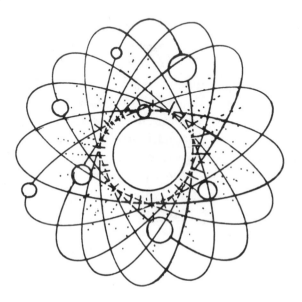

It is the nucleus that also has the capacity for a multidimensional communication. It is the core that differentiates itself
from the parts as a higher intelligent function with both the
capacity to reach into the unconscious mechanisms of the
organism and the capacity to communicate with higher dimension of the Self. Thus the nucleus has the very special role of
receiving and transmitting higher intention. It, in fact, connects the being with all that is below and above.

Embracing the principle of Nucleation gives us permission to
allow for the differentiation of a special part within ourselves,
within a group, or within the human community. In an
evolving being, a nucleus will come forth to assume a central
role.

> **We can search for and identify a center**
> **within ourselves, and we can choose to be-**
> **come part of the emerging planetary**
> **nucleus.**

We, Humanity, have the potential to co-ordinate Gaia's bodily functions, establish communication with other planetary beings, and, if we are especially playful, become the very ETA itself, just to see what will happen.

Chapter 6

THE FABRIC OF LOVE
Principles of Relationship

Four principles demonstrate fundamental processes of relationship between the part and the whole. These principles describe the way things are, or *can be*, depending on how we choose to view our reality and to live our lives.

Synergy describes the release of free energy that occurs when a group of entities come together with a common aim. *Attunement* occurs when an individual being tunes to and invokes resonance with a higher order of reality. *Alignment* occurs when an individual chooses to find meaning and purpose in

77

contributing to the wellbeing or evolution of a larger reality. *Quantum transformation* is the miraculous process of discreet, unpredictable leaps in level of integration and consciousness.

Synergy

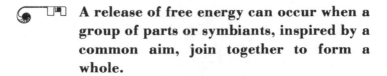

A release of free energy can occur when a group of parts or symbiants, inspired by a common aim, join together to form a whole.

Synergy is one step up from symbiosis. In symbiosis parts join together for mutual support, each part attempting to enhance itself by joining in the creation of a nurturing environment. It is just here, however, that a miracle occurs. In proper relationship, when the experiment works, each part not only receives what it needs for life support but also receives energy for its own enhancement. In addition there is further free energy that is available for the work of the whole organism. Exactly how this occurs is still a mystery to science.

This is the experience of love. "When two or more are joined together in my name, there shall I be." This is the magical release of potential that springs forth whenever just the right group of elements or people come together.

The whole is both quantitatively and qualitatively greater and more wonderful than the sum of its parts.

From whence came the additional energy? From within, from above, or created directly by the force of love?

Synergic release is often experienced in the beginning of group work. An alchemical fusion occurs, at least momentarily, when individuals come together. A high is experienced, a new sense of self-transcendent being. It is just this free energy that can be directed toward evolutionary work.

The principle of Synergy describes the evolutionary process by which greater and greater levels of integration occur. Synergic release from wave/particle formations led to the creation of the atom; atomic combinations resulted in molecules; molecules in organelles; organells in cells, etc. At each new union an attractive force is released that seeks out the next evolutionary stage of union.

One of the classic examples in Western cultures of the potency of synergy is found in the amazing, transformative architecture of the Gothic cathedrals (Charpentier, 1972). Over hundreds of years individual monks joined together in group work dedicated to the service of God. The results went beyond the enhancement of their personal spiritual experience and the continuation of their orders. There was also a significant piece of evolutionary work—the Gothic cathedral, a symbol of transformation, a sacred space, a place intentionally designed to provide conditions for transformational experiences.

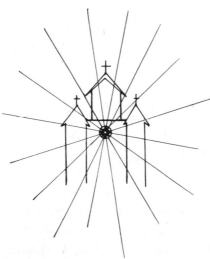

Understanding Synergy allows us to participate in group
work without fear of being absorbed or of losing our individuality. A word of caution, however: if group members are asked
to sacrifice their unique and true individuality, the group
endeavor may be wrongly directed. If, on the other hand,
individuality is enhanced and deepened by the group relationship, a genuine vehicle for evolutionary work may be occurring.

Knowledge of the principle of Synergy gives direction to our
search for next steps in the evolutionary adventure.

**Beyond the capacities of the individual,
the group, properly configured, properly
supported by its members, and well
blessed from above, may be the vehicle for
transmitting high-level energies necessary
for the emergence of a new age.**

The group may well be the next level of evolutionary being
beyond the individual. The group may provide the next stepping stone toward the unification of humankind.

Attunement

**Deep peace and mutual nurturance can
occur when a resonant harmonic relationship is established between an individual
evolving being and a greater reality.**

True attunement is a voluntary and conscious process
initiated by the individual who openly responds to a call from
within. Attunement is an expression of receptive will in which
the larger consciousness is invited and permitted to penetrate
more and more deeply into self-consciousness. In this way

individual energies are attuned to the Universe just as a musical instrument is tuned to the dominant key of an orchestral theme.

An instrument out of attunement would sound cacophonous and harsh and would clearly be disruptive to the aim of the group. While an individual, society or culture may insist on a way of being—a psychic set or life style—that maintains a non-resonant relationship with the environment, such a disharmony must ultimately have serious implications for both the part and the whole.

Healing as an art/science in traditional Peruvian culture springs from a quite different perspective than our contemporary medical practices (although current holistic health approaches do tend in this direction). Illness, in general, is viewed and diagnosed as a vibrational imbalance between the individual and the environment. Healing then seeks to *reattune* the specific individual energy field with the particular environmental field in which the person is presently living. Hence diagnosis and remedy will differ according to the environmental forces with which the person is to attune.

All of the great spiritual traditions of the past as well as the variety of consciousness activities that have appeared during the last 25 years are ways of attunement. All forms of meditation may be said to be practices of attunement to a deeper, higher or more inner consciousness.

Right understanding of the principle of attunement validates and adds deeper meaning to our work of personal transformation. There is a definite limit to how much we are willing to do for our individual selves—the frame of reference is too small. However, as we come to see that a work of internal attunement with a larger reality also serves evolution, we then have the necessary inspiration to continue our work in good conscience.

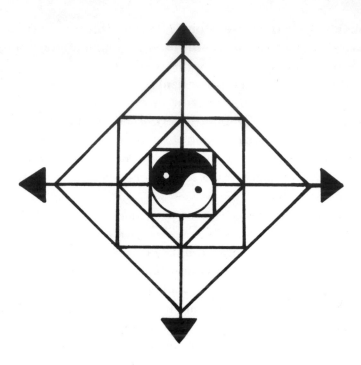

Alignment

 The wellbeing of all is enhanced when an individual part consciously chooses to serve the evolution of the whole.

For the most part, the work of alignment on the deepest levels is invisible. Thus we are able to recognize only a small degree of the beneficial influences that have resulted from the work of individuals, groups and esoteric schools over the ages. We can be sure, however, that the positive aspects of our current culture and consciousness are not the result of evolutionary accident.

In the more visible world, however, there are numerous examples of alignment. In each case an individual or group has chosen to align their life with a higher purpose. The theoretical and practical discoveries of enlightened scientific inquiry have just begun to serve their purpose. Through pushing the limits of our understanding of the basic elements of matter, we have come to an impasse. We now recognize that we cannot know all that we wish to know. We are forced to seek creative solutions that include a receptivity to other realms of non-rational knowledge.

The work of great spiritual teachers also expresses the activity of alignment. The current experimental city and community of Auroville is a direct result of the teaching of Sri Aurobindo. This, however, is but a small part of the influence he will have on our future evolution. Similarly, the influence of G.I. Gurdjieff will have subtle yet profound effects upon our subsequent development. After years of travel in Central Asia in search of ancient, practical methods of transformation, Gurdjieff developed a system of ideas and practices that are now studied by individuals and groups throughout the world. Similarly, many other remarkable teachers have inspired millions of people to seek for a deeper sense of themselves and for a sense of purpose in their lives.

How does one determine the life course that will bring alignment? Perhaps a person does not decide on his or her life's work, but rather discovers it. It has even been suggested that:

The discovery of one's purpose is the rediscovery of a promise made by the soul prior to incarnation.

Alignment is the path of the Bodhisattva. Alignment is active will in the service of conscious evolution.

Quantum Transformation

 In each evolving being, the nucleus works toward turning the attention of a significant percentage of the parts toward evolutionary transformation. When this percentage is reached (critical mass), the idea is transmitted rapidly and directly to all parts of the organism, and a quantum evolutionary leap is experienced.

The principle of Quantum Transformation offers us hope. All the stubborn parts of oneself do not have to agree to change and grow. All the people of the world do not have to join in the work of planetary transformation. Evolution is possible.

Suppose I am making some sauce, like a hollandaise, which is liable to demulsify—that is, the butter separates from the egg. This can be a terrifying experience if you are making sauce for sixty or seventy people with pounds of butter and dozens of eggs. An inexperienced cook loses his head and beats the sauce violently—but only makes things worse. A good cook pours a little water at one edge of the bowl and stirs quietly until it turns back again, and then it spreads through the whole mass until the sauce is right again. The first time you do this, it seems almost miraculous. It is the same with the world. Everywhere people are stirring so violently to get oil and water to mix. This cannot happen. The part of wisdom is to establish, here and there, centers in which right relationship can exist by the power of a common understanding of what is ultimately important. From such centers there

> can spread throughout the world—perhaps
> more quickly than you might imagine possible
> —the seeds of a new world.   (Bennet, 1973:50)

There we have it. Just a little nudge here, and the whole thing moves. We have also playfully called this the "monkey-root principle," based on the often-heard tale of a certain group of monkeys that live on a series of islands off the coast of Japan. The story has it that one day a young monkey decided to wash his potato, rather than eat it dirty as was the custom. Having found this delectable and delicious, he went right ahead and told a few other monkeys of his amazing discovery. One by one, the monkeys on the island adopted this washing game and found they enjoyed their potatoes more than ever before. At last, there was only one monkey left, a recalcitrant old fellow, who bluntly rejected the experiment. He would do things his own way. However, in time he too decided to give it a try, as he noticed the wellbeing and enthusiasm of his compatriots. On the day that he adopted this practice, it just so happened that all the monkeys on the adjoining islands simultaneously commenced washing their potatoes! A quantum transformation— the monkey-root principle. It took just that last stubborn fellow to turn the tide, just that last little bit of energy to complete the thought, and presto! the pattern emerges *in toto*.

What miraculous process is at work here? How is it that the part can change the whole with just a little nudge? Perhaps there is a bit of magic—the magic of hidden inclination or instruction. Perhaps the intention to be transformed lies deep within the being of every little part. Was it born there—an evolutionary inclination—or was it absorbed from hidden higher sources through secret subtle channels?

On the one hand, the "internal factors in evolution," (Whyte, 1969), the inherent tendency to evolve, urges us toward complexity, toward greater consciousness, toward Divine reunion.

**It takes only a clear and definite sugges-
tion from one small part to remind the
rest of its inborn preference for evolution.**

So it may have been way back then, when a few cells here and
there divided into two to try the dance of union, that suddenly
all of thě cells remembered their potential for multiplication
and magnificence.

On the other hand, a guiding intelligence, a teaching from
within, may be given and received. An inner ear begins to hear
the call, begins to sense the possibility; a responsive inclination
awakens and readies itself for transformation. The way to
change is seen, the pattern recognized. Perhaps this was the
case when the call to life was heard throughout the molecular
body of Gaia. Just a little life was born, and all the rest
responded.

It is said by those who practice transcendental meditation
that when just a small percentage of the people of a city practice meditation, a marked decrease in crime results—as if even

the hardest criminals know deep within of a better way to be. Yet, a subtle suggestion is needed—a sounding of the dominant chord—to remind us of the harmony that we already know to be.

It is just this way with each of us. We often hold onto a belief or behavior for a very long time. Until one day a very subtle thing—an idea or song—initiates a change that affects our whole life.

It is difficult, to be sure, to imagine all of Humanity transforming in a moment to a state of respect and service. However, it is not so difficult to recognize that:

If a small yet critical percentage of **Humanity is able to see the light, there will be intonations and ramifications for all of the human family.**

An Opening

Within universal evolution there are many levels. Each of us has the potential to participate in conscious evolution. This is done by self-study, transformational practices and alignment with the greater process of planetary evolution.

Gaia, the living Earth, has her own evolution to attend to. We are part of her process and she is part of us. Gaia in turn participates in the evolution of even greater celestial systems.

We face today the challenge of understanding the planetary context in which we have our being and of participating as fully as possible in the conscious evolution of our world.

PART III

DIMENSIONS OF EVOLUTION

Chapter 7: **Personal Transformation**
The evolution of the individual follows a
path similar to planetary evolution. Help
is available and may be accepted.

Chapter 8: **Planetary Transformation**
Gaia, at midlife, seeking self-integration,
aspires to call together the parts of her
being into one harmonious whole. Within
her slumbers humankind, her developing
self-consciousness.

Chapter 9: **Gaia in the Living Universe**
As a member of the solar family and the
galactic conference, Gaia participates in
cosmic evolution. The scale is so vast that
we humans stand in awe.

Chapter 10: **The Challenge Before Us**
We are aware at this moment in evolutionary history of great distress and great
possibility. We begin to respond by shifting our mode of perception from one of
limitation to one of potential. The Challenge is then to act accordingly in every
realm of human activity.

Chapter 7

PERSONAL TRANSFORMATION

The potentials of the individual human being are perhaps unlimited—wed as we are to a universe of limitless possibilities. Still we must start at the beginning and deal with ourselves as we are.

The focus will be on one lifetime. Theories of the evolution of the soul over many lifetimes will be left to others of deeper understanding. The task of envisioning the potentials of one life seems adequately complex for now. This chapter outlines one specific way of approaching personal transformation. The treatment is summary, intended to indicate broad patterns and possibilities, rather than to offer specific applicable methods.

Childhood and early adult development occur as a consequence of the interactions between the innate wisdom of the young individual and environmental influences—parents, peers, natural environment, cultural values, etc. Very little real growth or change is initiated by the personal consciousness. However, as Carl Jung has pointed out, the second half of life presents an array of entirely different possibilities.

Centered around the search for the Self, the second half of life explores and embraces the inner worlds, brings synthesis to a person's understanding, and offers the opportunity for self-initiated conscious evolution.

Many models of personal transformation are available. This one has been selected because it places individual growth in an evolutionary context. Included are five primary stages of development: identification, acceptance, coordination, integration and synthesis.* These sequential growth processes overlap and interpenetrate with the stages of personal harmonization, transpersonal realization and conscious evolutionary service as discussed in Chapter 2. Roughly, the following match applies:

Identification	
Acceptance	Personal Harmonization
Coordination	
Integration	Transpersonal Realization
Synthesis	Conscious Evolutionary Service

---

*This schema is derived from psychosynthesis. The present interpretation differs somewhat from the original, verbally given material.

Personal transformation starts with a question about myself and my potential. Such a question can be stimulated by pain, joy or ennui. In any case a search into the unknown realm of self begins at that very special moment when I realize that I myself must initiate this change. Once this realization has penetrated, there is no way out. The process has begun and my life has opened to an additional dimension.

Unconscious Evolution

In the early prenatal stage of life, the entire evolution of humankind is available for observation—ontogeny recapitulating phylogeny. Unconscious personal evolution begins at conception, when the sperm finds its way to the secret chamber of the ovum. There they are joined in holy matrimony, forever after to be one. During the uterine period, the cells, organs and limbs are formed. Then the quantum transformation of birth— an entirely new reality. Interaction with the outer world begins now, and therefore, the development of personality (or, more accurately, personalities). Fortunately there is help from above —just as there always has been for young humankind. An inner guiding wisdom keeps watch, influencing, teaching and nurturing whenever possible.

The young being now passes through the formative years wherein the physical body grows, the emotional nature becomes defined and the intellectual mind develops. Relative to our potential for conscious choice, this is a reactive period.

Somewhere in mid-life (25-50 years), for those who wish, a marked change can occur. The physical organism, having reached its peak, now begins a gradual decline toward death. Simultaneously, however, just at this time of apparent demise, new potentials for conscious self-development appear. These include the refinement of the emotional being, the sharpening of mental capacities, and the opening of energy channels (the antahkarana or rainbow bridge) to the deeper dimensions of the Self.

Some traditional models of spiritual growth begin by immediately attempting to establish a connection between the outer person and the Higher Self. This approach bypasses the problems of personality. However, a number of contemporary models of transformation offer a more holistic picture that pays respect to all aspects of the person, including the outer egoistic parts. Thus (as outlined in Chapter 2) the developmental pattern offered here begins with the harmonization of the personality, then proceeds to the establishment of subtle connections with the spiritual nature, and finally reaches the stage of planetary service—conscious evolution.

For a healthy person in mid-life, the physical body is primarily cared for by the inner wisdom, with only a modest amount of attention required from the outer self.

Psychological wellbeing and growth, however, is a definite challenge for those who wish to evolve. The responsibility of self-transformation rightfully belongs to each of us.

While this is especially true in contemporary Western culture, it is not always the case. In highly structured tribal societies, for example, the psychological, social and spiritual needs of the individual are for the most part cared for by the socio-religious fabric. With the exception of selected individuals who are called to penetrate the mysteries and become Shamans, most individual growth occurs spontaneously and unconsciously. However, the age of unconscious group being is passing. We are now called to develop ourselve on all levels and to establish direct relationship to the process of planetary evolution. The task begins.

What is the situation for most of us in the West? Gurdjieff's
imagery is potent. We are fast "asleep," caught in "false personality," caught in an image of ourselves and unable to alter
or change it. All of our reactions are "mechanical." This perspective very much mirrors the classic behaviorist point of
view, in which we are seen solely as the consequence of external
influences. However, Gurdjieff radically differs from the
behaviorist perspective as to what is possible. For him the
human being is a noble creature, with profound potentials.
Nonetheless, at present there is a great difference between ourselves as we are and as we have the potential to be.

A group of friends recently traveled to Los Angeles and were
picked up by a cab driver who told of an interesting past as a
once well-known jazz musician. As the conversation progressed,
he turned out to be quite lively and entertaining. He was
involved in writing a book and a number of other creative
projects. In the course of the conversation, he confessed that
this was an unusual exchange and that he experienced most of
his customers as literally dead. In spite of his gentle probing to
initiate an interesting conversation, they were usually com-
pletely unavailable. His interpretation was that they were
absolutely controlled by their image of themselves, and that a
real exchange with a cab driver did not fit this image. Being

unable to avail themselves of him, they missed an opportunity
for a meaningful human communication. This piece of
wisdom, appearing in an everyday context, reflects Gurdjieff's
notion of mechanical Humanity. It's good to know, therefore,
that there is hope.

Beginning to Awaken

The first moment of awakening may be a difficult one as it
challenges my beliefs about who and how I am. This is the
moment of realizing that there is little or no true center in
myself. I am driven by external circumstances and directed by
predetermined behavioral patterns. This realization is likely to
engender a state of disease, that is, "dis-ease," a great discon-
tent with myself. I may be inclined to run from this, to say
"Oh, well, that's not the case" and to reconstitute my image
of myself as a self-initiating being. However, it is said
that *the only way out is through*—to face this truth and to
deepen my perception of it. This very confrontation is the beginning of self-consciousness.

Initiation to this experience comes in a variety of ways: a
recognized and acknowledged sense of ennui or boredom; an
acute experience of pain, wherein I see my personal failure and
my inability to change; or a moment of inspiration, a peak
experience wherein I taste deeply a way of being that is qualitatively different from anything hitherto experienced. From the
vantage point of such a special moment, it is possible to see
and acknowledge the normal state of affairs in which I usually
live. This is the first awakening. This is a subtle quantum
transformation from complete sleep to profound question, from
superficial self-defense or self-assertion to deep self-inquiry.

If now I have the courage to admit that, in spite of all my
efforts, there has been no real change, and I know not where or

how to proceed, a great illumination occurs. Perhaps I can be helped—a moment of humility.

There are a number of sources of help, within and without, around and above. Great literature can bring illumined inspiration. Friends and colleagues who have similarly faced this question can be a source of guidance. A psychotherapist or counselor, a guru or teacher. This, then, is a time of penetration, of allowing influences from without to act upon the tidily woven complex of my personality.

Something, someone must take charge of this search. Who shall it be?

In a dream, I found myself at a country retreat, a meeting center where I was warmly and ceremoniously greeted by an elegant, elderly gentleman who obviously was the host and director. However, on waking the next morning (still within the dream), I found that this centrally important person had jumped into his Cadillac and left, leaving the whole operation without guidance. The remaining staff began to quarrel, and soon everything was chaos. Clearly a new guiding element was needed for the community. In retrospect, this dream suggests the abdication of the ego, a false center, a subsequent state of chaos, and a renewed search for guidance and direction.

What, then, is the rightful role of the counselor or teacher to whom I go for help? Certainly not to control the transformation. The real direction will come from within. Rather, to be a friend, while a quieter, deeper part of myself comes forward to lead the search. The guide will wait and watch, encourage and question, but never pre-empt the initiative. In this way, a contact can be established, not with the hitherto controlling ego, but rather with a part of myself that truly wishes for transformation. In the beginning, this part is very small and has not a great deal of influence—this fledgling nucleus. But in time it will develop force and become a channel and source of guidance.

Now that I know what is possible, I accept responsibility for

self-healing and avail myself of whatever support can come
from within and without. From a state of unconscious attachment to my self-image, I now proceed to the practice of conscious *identification* of the parts of personality. Along with the
recognition of sleep comes the realization that "I" am many,
rather than one. With the dissolution of my self-image, I notice
that there are a variety of personalities, or subpersonalities,
present within my loosely configured self.

> The functions of an individual, in whom
> various psychological traits are not integrated,
> form what we consider to be sub-personalities. . .
> One discovers how very different and often
> quite antagonistic traits are displayed in the
> different roles. . . Ordinary people shift from
> one to the other without clear awareness, and
> only a thin thread of memory connects them;
> but for all practical purposes they are different
> beings—they act differently, they show very
> different traits.   (Assagioli, 1965:75)

The first stage of work now begins as a newborn self-
consciousness observes and identifies the parts of myself. The
observation must be non-controlling, non-changing, a quiet
watching with no attempt to eliminate or alter what I see. A
negatively regarded subpersonality at this point may represent
only a superficial expression of a deeply valuable talent. For
example, to do away with judgmentalness might also eliminate
the profoundly important quality of critical discrimination.
Also, there is the danger of cutting short the expression of an
energy that is at least integrated into the current homeostatic
pattern. Cut off from its accustomed channel, this unconscious
emotional energy will seek expression wherever possible, perhaps in dangerously unintegrated ways, such as depression or
fanaticism.

This is also the period of the discovery of "I," that special human quality that sees without attachment, that seeks to understand human nature with deep compassion. The emergent, conscious "I" now studies each subpersonality. First the behavior is identified, then the attitudes, and then the deeper values wherein the behavior originates. A deep penetration is required in order to discover the function that each subpersonality believes it is serving in the interest of the whole—its own sense of purpose. This is a long and difficult process. The basic reasons for the roles I play are often quite opposite to the motivations I believe are moving me.

If I am easily hurt by others, it may be because I already hurt within myself. This is a way of self-nurturance, of allowing myself to feel my sadness. Another part that expresses great self-assurance may be covering and protecting a deep sense of vulnerability. Another subpersonality may express itself in a "bitchy" fashion, a behavior in which I have no direct interest whatsoever. This pattern may have been copied from my mother or father—the child unconsciously attempting to be in the world in an "appropriate" manner, as modeled by the parent.

As I am able to tap deeply into the meaning of each subpersonality, the next stage unfolds: *acceptance*. No part is unworthy of inclusion in the whole, only the outer manifestations may require remodeling. As the subpersonalities are mutually accepted by a central consciousness, they spontaneously begin to align themselves with one another, and negative, self-destructive behaviors spontaneously begin to fall away. Positive, constructive behaviors, that fulfill the same basic needs, now begin to emerge, and a harmonious *coordination* (third stage) of the personality results. During this period, two important processes are occurring simultaneously: the harmonization or coordination of the personalities, and the birth of self-consciousness.

An additional process commences at this point—the birth of

individual will. As the parts begin to coordinate spontaneously, the coordinative center, the "I," now starts to actively participate in the harmonizing process, withdrawing attention from a quality here, accenting a quality there, creating a harmonious field. In this way, the will begins to serve an integrative function. Here is the birth of a nucleus, a center, with a growing ability to co-create the configuration of the personality. This nuclear "I," having established some degree of authority, is now prepared for further exploration into the establishment of communication with deeper dimensions of consciousness.

Spiritual Realization

Having coordinated the subpersonalities (and of course it is never so neat and tidy out here in real life), a higher order of *integration* (fourth stage) becomes possible. Herein the previously conflicting parts of myself now willingly cooperate and lend their intentions toward the task at hand. I, as a collective entity, now work toward the attunement of my individual consciousness with the larger energy field. However, in the beginning only some parts of the personality choose this unification, while others still remain unconvinced that harmonic relationship with the whole will be a more nurturing condition than egocentricity. Various practices of meditation are available to help in this work of quieting the personal energy field, of becoming more responsive to the harmonic attraction of the larger energy field. This, then, is the work of attunement, of spiritual realization.

This is the development of receptive will, an act of reception rather than doing or changing. This is a practice of permission, of allowing myself to be influenced and harmonized by something greater. Although many, many volumes have been written on the work of spiritual realization, little of a general nature can be said. This task is a highly personal one, and appropriate methods differ for each of us.

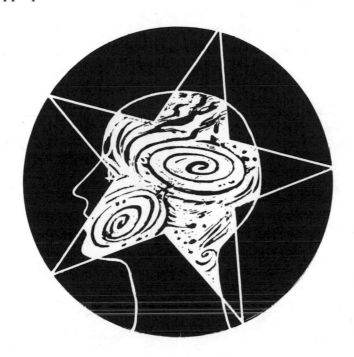

Spiritual realization is a work of opening **the attention to that which eternally is.**

The quest for spiritual realization is, of course, a long, often difficult, yet ultimately enriching process. As harmonic attunement proceeds, a further work presents itself. From deep within myself comes forth the question: for what have I worked all these years? Is there a meaning beyond my personal realization? With this question commences the fifth stage of *synthesis*. Herein the integrated subpersonalities, directed by a central self, choose to participate in conscious evolution.

Chapter 8

PLANETARY TRANSFORMATION

We know not how long fetal Earth may have been dwelling in the womb before birth, or in what form or manner she was conceived. Our metascience says Gaia was born of the solar family, a child of evolutionary intention, an expression of divine experiment. Our science estimates that she was born some 4 1/2 billion years ago. From the ether, to gas, to mineral matter—a physical being at first, without apparent life. Some 3 1/2 billion years ago simple, unicellular life awakened and the biosphere was born. Since then organic life has been evolving in myriad, diverse forms. All are part of one being—the living biosphere. We have long known that this being, Gaia, is alive and well.

Some say high cultures (such as Egypt, Peru, Butan and Atlantis) may have flourished as long as 50,000-100,000 years. The ancients of these past and even forgotten civilizations not only respected and revered Gaia, but even devoted enormous energy to the construction of stone (crystaline) monuments which served to receive, transform and distribute extra-terrestrial energies (Michell, 1969). In this way these ancient learned beings were able not only to pay their dues, as it were, but even to contribute to the wellbeing and evolution of Gaia.

For many millenia humankind knew the planet to be a living being, capable of great wisdom and worthy of worship. This understanding of Gaia and the related geomantic sciences however has almost entirely disappeared from our consciousness, or shall we say, has receded into deep hiding within our unconscious. However. . .

The Gaia Hypothesis

In 1975 a most remarkable bit of speculative science came our way. The publication of the Gaia Hypothesis (Lovelock and Epton, 1975) offered for the first time a scientifically-based synthesis of geophysical research and ancient tradition regarding the nature of Gaia. It was a wonderful surprise when our Western mind first formulated the **Gaia Hypothesis** stating that we will do very well indeed to regard Gaia as a living self-regulative organism.

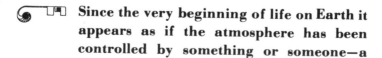 **Since the very beginning of life on Earth it appears as if the atmosphere has been controlled by something or someone—a**

self-regulatory intelligence, an evolutionary intention, a guiding wisdom—that has
demonstrated its ability by controlling
atmospheric conditions in just exactly the
way necessary for the survival and evolution of life.

Evidence supporting the Gaia Hypothesis comes from two
primary sources. The first is the constancy of temperature for
the past 3 1/2 billion years, within the range of 15-30 degrees
centigrade. These are the only thermal conditions (between
freezing and boiling) in which life can survive. Quite remark-

able, this sure and steady self-control. According to speculations that take into account a marked increase in solar radiation, planetary temperature should have climbed to intolerable heights. Remarkable indeed, Gaia found a way—microbiological production of heat-retaining gases—to keep cool.

The second source of evidence supporting the Gaia Hypothesis has been the consistent atmospheric composition of high oxygen content (just the right proportion for life). This began some two billion years ago (not so coincidentally, it appears) at just the right time, when microbiological organisms that feed on oxygen were evolving. Or, was it vice-versa? No one knows. Remarkably, however, this highly oxygenated, life-supportive atmosphere has remained constant ever since. This evidence turns upside down our long-held scientific picture of organic life on Earth struggling for survival in an inorganic and indifferent atmosphere! From the perspective of the Gaia hypothesis it looks as if the very opposite is true—that the biosphere actively controls atmospheric conditions, with the wellbeing of life in mind.

With the clearing of our vision, an ancient, living wisdom, capable of making judgments and initiating change in the service of evolution seems self-evident. This guiding wisdom is analogous to the unconscious wisdom of the individual body— a highly refined, subtle, efficient consciousness capable of a variety of responses to an equally large variety of influences or environmental changes.

Humankind and Gaia

We come now to the evolution of humankind. What role shall we play in the evolution of the planetary being? Epton and Lovelock offer one suggestion:

We are sure that man needs Gaia, but could
Gaia do without man? In man Gaia has the
equivalent of a central nervous system, and the
awareness of herself and the rest of the universe. Through man she has a rudimentary
capacity, capable of development, to anticipate
and guard against threats to her existence. For
example, man can command just about enough
capacity to ward off a collision with a planetoid
the size of Icarus. Can it then be that in the
course of man's evolution within Gaia, he has
been acquiring the knowledge and skills necessary to insure her survival?   (1975:306)

In this vision, Humanity has the important, yet humble role
of stewardship.

In symbiotic, harmonious relationship with
the innate wisdom of Gaia, we, Humanity,
will provide a new category of response
mechanism, capable of neutralizing the
effects of our civilizations on the natural
environment and of protecting Gaia,
through the use of technology, from
unforeseen cosmic threats.

Humankind will indeed play a significant role in the future
when we recognize our place and pay proper homage to Gaia,
the mother of our physical and psychological self. ·
   What other meanings can we see in humankind's evolution in
Gaia? Teilhard de Chardin, with great poetic vision, sees that
"A glow ripples outward from the first spark of conscious
reflection." This is the thinking layer, the "noosphere," the
mind of Humanity weaving a psychic fabric to claim our given
birthright.

To give man his true place in nature it is not
enough to find one more pigeon-hole in the
edifice of our systemization or even an additional order or branch. With hominization, in
spite of the insignificance of the anatomical
leap, we have the beginning of a new age. The
earth 'gets a new skin.' Better still, it finds its
soul.

(Teilhard, 1965:182)

From both the speculations of rational inquiry and the vision
of mystical insight, Humanity steps forward to play a role in
the evolution of planetary consciousness. We are indeed of
great importance, or should be, shall we say. She has great
hopes for us, her offspring. She has been long in preparing our
cradle, longer still in building our home.

At the very beginning when Gaia was born it was necessary
for her to identify and differentiate herself in solar space. She
then developed a "membrane," the ozone layer to contain the
life within, and to filter influences from without which might
be too strong for her sensitive inner life. The egoistic membrane, it could appropriately be called. Within her, a dynamic,
vital, brilliantly self-nurturing unity pulses each day in
response to the soft caresses of the sun. At the same time, slow
dying occurs all about her body as involution claims its toll.
And right within the same biospheric tissue, God and Human-
kin work for evolution. Perpetual transcendence can be noted
in every pulsing day. Correspondence is visible in every dimension—from atomic cell to planetary electron, from transcendent
individuality to the emergent Being of Humanity.

Around about mid-life Gaia has decided to nucleate, to call
forth from her bowels an evolutionary being—the ETA.
Humankind appears, to fumble its way forward toward an
unknown future. This now-becoming entity, the Human Being

to be, will be full of magnificence and play as it assumes its rightful role in planetary life and evolution.

This nucleation has been a long, slow and often difficult process, laced with pain and anguish. Slowly we remember our purpose. Gradually we realize that our strength is *for something*, rather than against. Gaia needs Humanity to help soothe her sorrows and realize her Self. But before such service is possible much human learning and growth is necessary, a profound transformation is required.

What then will the evolution of humankind look like as we awaken to our potential? Today we cannot help but see a world of pain and disease, torn by the madness of emnity and war. We look upon ourselves and see there is no nucleus, no unifying center. We see a multitude of peoples—of separate personalities. Only faint suggestions of coordination are discernable—Christianity, the United Nations, the scientific community, the New Age consciousness. All are attempts to unify and to bring peace among us. Yet, at present, there is still no integration apparent to our ordinary perceptual vision. We must look more deeply then.

Those of us who know of our potential must begin to look into the heart of each people, each group, each person. We must learn to identify and honor both the sincerity and variety of human aspiration. As we proceed we will begin to see that "The American Way," the American consciousness will bring one vital quality to the being of Humanity, while the consciousness of the Chinese, the Arabs and the Australian Aborigines will each make its unique contribution. In this way the differentiated parts someday will come to respect and support one another. Soon we will come to recognize that our common task is a trans-human one, a goal beyond ourselves. The hubris of Humanity is surely part of the difficulty. We have yet to mature enough to seek meaning beyond our own needs and desires. Yet soon we will awaken—we are awakening, this very moment.

⚜⚜⚜

Help is on the Way

With a purpose higher than ourselves, integration begins, along with the coordination of the parts—harmony among people of the Earth, peace on earth, goodwill toward men and women. How shall this come to pass? We see, as did the individual upon first realization of waking sleep, that our resources are limited, our values askew. We look for help both within and without. Is there a wise counselor available, or perhaps an ancient sage?

Help is in fact available. Many people have opened themselves to serve as channels for that which is deep in the human psyche—the everpresent, traditional teaching of old. In 1970 David Spangler received a series of transmissions, which he describes as a "communion with an impersonal consciousness that identified itself through the qualities of Limitless Love and Truth."

> That which occurs now upon the earth is the reception of a new maturity of consciousness. If you would receive it you must change and become mature, adults under spiritual law. . .
>
> That which I represent and that which I call forth from within you is timeless. Your maturity has been with you since the beginning of your creation. You cannot lose it; you will all gain it one day; and that day, for those who can accept, is here now. Through a transformed humanity, creating a new heaven and a new earth, and through the force, maturity and openness of their consciousness allowing the presence of this new heaven and new earth to manifest itself, the earth that you have known will change and transfigure itself into matching beauty. Therefore let my revelation be one of hope, one of joy, one of love and one of truth.
>
> (1976:82)

This is just one of many such revelations, and of course we will receive them with caution and wonder. From whence do they come? Are they ill or well-intentioned? How shall we judge their validity? In spite of our suspicions of subjective projections and astral injections, we *are* beginning to pay attention. We are listening for messages of guidance from every possible source: tuning in our astro-radios, talking to dolphins, and listening more and more attentively to the words of those among us with psychic abilities. Is there help out there? Is there guidance in here? Will anyone respond?

"Yes" is the response, loud and clear—surprisingly with a

good bit of general consensus. We are in the midst of a tremendous transition in human/planetary evolution. The things of old are going out through the ozone—depart the egosphere. No more time for little people with gigantic self-images hiding nothing in particular. A time of union and harmony is upon us.

Reports vary·on the degree of upheaval accompanying the change, ranging from wintery depression to earth-quaking disaster. But we shall pass through, we shall be born anew. At least, that is, those who care, the children of the dawn.

Humans have recognized the need for help throughout the ages, and have found a response in the teachings of the prophets. The transmissions of these prophets (Christ, Mohammed, Buddha, etc.) later formed the bases for the world's great religions. Our misinterpretations of these ideas of personal salvation and enlightenment have resulted in a good bit of suffering. Nonetheless, in spite of the difficulties, these religions have brought to us deep wisdom teachings that have in general enlightened and uplifted humankind in our gradual ascent toward the forthcoming new age.

We now enter a period wherein the goal of individual salvation is no longer appropriate. Our guidance calls for a collective transformation. The dispersed elements of the Human Being cry for a self-healing that is guided by deep inner wisdom.

Humanity Awakening

The present recognition of our emergent collective consciousness represents a quantum transformation in human evolution. During the first part of the Twentieth Century, a few pioneer thinkers, such as Teilhard and Gurdjieff, called our attention to our role in evolution. This ushered in an entirely new era. Humanity now begins to differentiate from other species on the planet in a unique way by taking responsibility for ourselves and for the planet. Just now we are ready to assume these responsibilities.

Students of evolution can easily perceive that the whole organism of Humanity will not assume responsibility simultaneously. Wars are still erupting on parts of the planet and crime is a common occurrence, in spite of a marked increase in global communication, global cooperation and global consciousness. We must and shall begin where we are. While much of human consciousness is still caught in a separative, alienated condition, significant numbers of individuals and groups are consciously working toward *critical mass*. When just the right quantity and quality of catalytic influence is reached, the entire process will be affected.

Everyone will not share the same realization at the same time. A part of Humanity will form the nucleus. At some special moment, as individual cells begin to relate as one, a

quantum leap will occur and the entire organism will quickly
cohere to a high level of integrity. Already there are a number
of groups—World Servers for the New Age, Planet Stewards,
Warriors of the Rainbow, Children of the Dawn, etc.—that
envision a unification of individual beings from all parts of
the planet as an evolutionary nucleus. The parts, the
individual cells that have already recognized their own function as planetary ETA, are being called together. They will
intuitively recognize one another.

Membership as far as we know is entirely open and inclusive. It is based on the inner development and the sincerity of
intention that each brings to the task of planetary evolution.
"Applications are being accepted, inquire within."

Many groups, working synergistically within themselves,
now have free energy available to influence and help others.
Further, we are beginning to see synergistic relationships
between these groups throughout the planet. Although we still
await integration on this level, a "network of light" is forming.

> True planetary leadership will emerge
> only when the glamour of leadership has
> been transcended, only when holding
> authority is seen as a sacred function
> offered in great humility.

With this will come a remembering of deep respect for wisdom.
The inner wisdom itself will be the actual center, the source of
unification around which a highly inspired, synergic group
will evolve.

What then is the planetary situation at the present moment?
The ancient self-regulatory wisdom of Gaia present since her
birth has been doing very well. Today, Gaia, at midlife,
seeking self-integration, aspires to call together the parts of her
being into one harmonic whole. Within her slumbers Humanity, a developing self-consciousness, still very much caught in

egoistic hubris, still very much self-concerned, imagining ourselves as separate from the context in which we live. But this limited understanding is soon to be transcended. A shift of attention will occur from the ego to that which cares deeply for Gaia. Hence we prepare ourselves, not only for planetary harmony but also for helping in the attunement of planetary consciousness to the all-embracing Universal Mind. This implies the recognition of Gaia's specific evolutionary function in the Universe. In the following chapter, theories that embrace this vast dimension of evolution are explored.

Chapter 9
GAIA IN THE LIVING UNIVERSE

Here and there in the vast endlessness of a living universe, tiny points of vibrant pulsation appear. Beings are born that will travel the journey toward conscious evolution.

Gaia, our mother Earth, may now be preparing for a step forward in evolution. And we, her children, seek to understand the magnificence. We have learned a good deal about her own development, but as to her role in the solar family, we know very little. Nonetheless, we have not failed to speculate at length.

117

Systems of knowledge regarding Gaia's role in the Universe differ greatly, both in their basic assumptions and in the resulting cosmologies. Thus, rather than offering a definitive answer, a question is posed. *How shall we come to regard her, what perspective shall we choose?* Diverse cosmologies reflect complementary aspects of the actual totality. By viewing sketches of them in relation to one another we can approach an understanding that will guide our choice.

Western Esotericism

The generic term "Western esotericism" encompasses a number of teachings which spring in essence from ancient esoteric tradition. These teachings have been rediscovered and expressed anew by a number of modern teachers, such as H.P. Blavatsky (1952), Rudolph Steiner (1970), and Alice A. Bailey (1962). From the esoteric perspective the Universe is seen fundamentally as consciousness in the process of evolution. All being and manifestation emanate from the Divine Source.

> The Monad, as we saw, is a spark of Divine Consciousness sensitive to the conditions upon its plane of manifestation; as soon as it gathers about itself a vehicle of matter of the plane below its own, it obscures its consciousness of its own plane but extends its consciousness to its vehicle; and so it proceeds down the planes till the physical body is developed.
>
> (Fortune, 1974:17)

From this lens we see consciousness descending into matter and, simultaneously, recalled through the evolution of higher and higher forms of consciousness.

The Earth then is one of the many places for the birth and
nurturance of consciousness. It is a meeting place, a place of
transformation of energy. In fact, in one esoteric perspective
(Powell, 1930) that is spelled out in more detail than most, the
physical planet as we know it is only one of 70 globes contained in the solar system. Only ten of these globes, however,
are said to be visible to human perception. The remaining 60
manifest on higher non-physical (astral, mental, buddhic and
atmic) planes. Groups of seven globes form what is called a
planetary chain. The totality of these chains form the "scheme
of evolution" of the solar system or Solar Logos. Thus the
evolution of the solar system, wherein "the physical Sun may
be considered as a sort of chakram or force center correspond-
ing to the heart of man. . ." (Powell, 1930:29), takes place in
multidimensional space, over long, long eons of time.

The Earth, as we know it, plays a small part but significant role, for at any one time only one globe in each chain is an active sphere for the evolution of consciousness. Gaia, just now, is the chosen location (of the Earth chain) for one such evolutionary experiment. And it is us, Humanity, that is regarded as the developing aspect of the planet. The system from which these notes spring penetrates deeply into both subatomic and cosmic creativity. Thus it goes far beyond the limits of our inquiry here. Suffice it to say that there has been much and varied study into the nature of our Mother Earth.

Another author, David Spangler, in a "Communication from an Angelic Source," introduces some key insights that reflect the esoteric perspective. This is quoted in some length, since to paraphrase would only reduce the clarity.

> Terra was set aside for the special task of being the purifier for your solar system for a period of time. Hence there were attracted to your world elements which I have mentioned of unresolved, unintegrated matter, energy and life to be harnassed into the denser nature of material form. Left in their exposed state, these energies had the power to impact harmfully upon the sensitive fabric of the solar Being and upon other planets and their life forms, being like a toxin within the systems of your own bodies. However, by being encapsulated into dense matter within the body of Terra, their vibrations could be slowed down and shielded from the body of the whole until these energies could be purified and reintegrated harmoniously and in love into the whole. . .
>
> Terra became a schoolhouse in the experience of confronting and resolving the challenges of primitive creativity and evolution. Your planet

became an arena for the interplay of the forces
of evolution on many levels and the forces of
non-integrated life and energy from many
sources, some quite primitive and others more
evolved, but all within a sidetrack of evolution
that placed these energies outside the communion of the whole. Thus Earth became
analogous to a kidney in the body of the solar
system, regulating and transmuting the energies
flowing throughout the system, removing im-
purities and returning to the body of the whole
only what is harmonious and integrated with
the progressive evolution of the whole. . .In this
fashion, your planet has performed a tremendous service to all lifestreams and all planetary
systems within the solar family, enabling them
to continue their patterns of development with
greater ease.

No planet or being is asked to perform such a
transmutative and sacrificial task endlessly,
nor is it allowed to do so. The time must come
when it takes up its own pattern of growth, new
service and development. Now Earth seeks and
is given this redemption in a vast initiatory
process occurring throughout the total body
and life of the Solar Father. . .

Now a vast work of purification is upon us to
cleanse and beautify Earth as one would
beautify a bride before her marriage; in this
fashion we greet Earth in her time of joy and
accomplishment. This event seeks its expression
through your hearts and minds and your dedi-
cation.

(1971:36-41)

From the esoteric then, Earth is seen both as a sacred being in transformation and as a place of transformation for individualized consciousness.

 Gaia has now reached the time in her evolutionary cycle when she can let go of her previous function and be transformed to a new and joyful mode of cosmic service.

We are in the process of entering the Age of Aquarius, the New Age.

The Cosmology According to Gurdjieff

As described by G.I. Gurdjieff (Ouspensky, 1949), the Universe is an integrated wholistic system, comprised of seven basic levels emanating from the Absolute. The system of categorization, called the ray of creation, includes the following levels, or dimensions: the Absolute, within this all worlds, within all worlds all suns, within all suns the sun, within the sun all planets, within all planets the earth, and within the earth the moon. This is our particular ray of creation—one among a multitude of rays (117,649 to be exact) that emanate from the Absolute. Down or out from the Absolute through the ray of creation into manifestation comes the basic universal energy in its involutionary expression. Thus, the Divine energy, decreasing in vibration and increasing in materialization, descends to the 7th lunar level. From there the return begins, the evolutionary process. This is the reclaiming of pure energy from the density of matter, the transformation to the pure vibrational field of the Absolute.

We see that the Earth is low in the ray of creation, far from the source. It is in the next to last place, on a remote tangent in a dark corner of the Universe. Conditions are very difficult here and we are subject to a great many mechanical laws.

Therefore, individual, human and planetary evolution on this plane is an extremely hard task worthy of our utmost respect.

We are potentially free beings; yet in our current sleep, little is possible. We must first awaken to our subjective, personal self and then to our objective, cosmic Self—which includes the being of Gaia.

The Earth itself is an evolving being, yet this unfoldment is a vast and slow process. Humanity's evolution as part of this process is equally slow, yet nonetheless necessary.

But the earth is also growing; not in the sense of size but in the sense of greater consciousness, greater receptivity. The planetary influences which were sufficient for her at one period of her existence become insufficient, she needs the reception of finer influences. To receive finer influences, a finer, more sensitive receptive apparatus is necessary. Organic life, therefore, has to evolve to adapt itself to the needs of the planets and the earth. . .

The evolving part of organic life is humanity. Humanity has also its evolving part but we will speak of this later; in the meantime we take humanity as a whole. If humanity does not evolve, it means the evolution of organic life would stop and this in turn would cause the growth of the ray of creation to stop. . .

(Ouspensky, 1949:305-306)

We see here the unified system of Gurdjieff in which each level of evolution is connected with all others. Humanity is intimately connected with the evolution of the Earth. Gaia, in turn, is integrally involved in the evolution of all other dimensions of the ray of creation. In his written works Gurdjieff did not identify a specific function that Earth may have in relation to the Solar System or Cosmos. He only noted that on this remote planet a number of errors have occurred that have seriously affected the life and sanity of the inhabitants. The human situation is therefore a difficult one. And, according to Gurdjieff, we can only hope to rectify it by radically changing ourselves. Only then will we possibly be able to participate consciously in the evolutionary process.

Gurdjieff's teachings are known as an expression of the Fourth Way—a way of inner development and work that appears and disappears during different phases of planetary history, according to when there is a specific need. Many believe that this teaching has been offered at present because of the importance of this specific moment in human and planetary evolution.

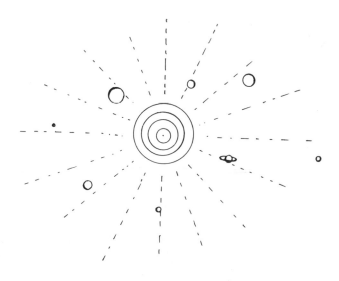

Western Science

Until very recently Western science has postulated the Universe as a mechanical system, and life on Earth as an artifact, an unrelated emergence, the result of accident and evolutionary mutation. This has transpired in spite of the fact that the problem of meaning has plagued science from the very beginning. Today, a unitive theory is being sought that responds to the long-felt need for including the phenomenon of consciousness.

From the scientific perspective, Earth has been seen astronomically as one of nine planets in the solar system, part of a galaxy which is one of a multitude of galaxies moving slowly away from each other into unknown isolation. However, as we begin to turn the corner, we adopt a broader and deeper vision.

> We are reminded of Prof. Eddington's comment that the stellar bodies appear to be strung out from the sun in specific 'mean' distances from one another, suggesting that when the gases constellated into planets they did so at a point of harmonic constriction—like musical scales— in obeyance to (as yet undetermined) laws of hierarchical order.
> (Blair, 1975:79)

This insight, along with many others in such fields as brain research, physics, geophysics and astronomy have upset our limited frame of reference. They have caused us to look again and to wonder at the subtlety of Gaia's "personal" relationships.

As quantum physics probes more and more deeply into subatomic phenomena (Capra, 1975) we find there. . .nothing of substance. Instead there are probabilities, relationships, wave phenomena, and harmonies. What's more, we find that nothing is independent of anything else. All is related; all is one.

As geophysics begins to recognize Gaia as a living entity, with her own internal self-regulatory systems, astronomy begins to recognize that Gaia is very much more related to the planets, the sun and the heavenly bodies than we ever before suspected. We begin to notice that the length of each day varies ever so slightly in response to subtle sunspot messages. (Gribbin, 1977)

We begin consciously to acknowledge an endearing love for and from the sun that we have always known, yet never quite been able to explain.

> Now it is understood that the sun and the earth
> are part of a much more closely integrated
> system. The earth is continuously immersed in
> a stream of charged particles flowing outward
> from the sun. This stream is called the "solar
> wind" and like the winds on earth, it is varia-
> ble, flowing sometimes very hard, sometimes
> softly.
>
>   (Young, 1977:183)

We begin to see that weather, seismic activity and even stress of human consciousness are influenced by not only the sun, but also by force fields and radiation from the planets, stars and other heavenly entities. We begin to recognize that there may be much to learn from the ancient art/science of astrology.

And yet, thus far, not a bit of all this fascinating rediscovery of intimate relationship responds to the question "Why?" We have not yet dared to look for purpose with our scientific eye. We are told that such speculation is not the job of science. But we can avoid it no longer.

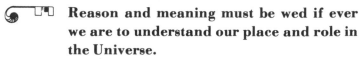 **Reason and meaning must be wed if ever we are to understand our place and role in the Universe.**

Chapter 10
THE CHALLENGE BEFORE US

The challenge we face today is immense—almost over-
whelmingly so. Two contrasting vistas present themselves. We
are aware at this point in evolutionary history of a great
distress upon and within Gaia, a metacrisis, and at the same
time, we are aware of a great possibility, a metapotential.
According to Peter Vajk, *Doomsday Has Been Cancelled*
(1978).

🐚 ⌐⌐ **We have the ability and the resources to turn the tide. We have the means within ourselves, Gaia, the solar system and the Universe to make it all work. Each of us can play a part. Each of us can make a contribution.**

This closing chapter touches on a few key ideas that help us align our personal visions with a larger vision. The first change we can make is to emphasize *what can be*, that is, to shift our mode of perception from one of limitation to one of potential.

Envisioning Ourselves

In viewing the very real problems with which we find ourselves confronted we can now acknowledge that *the way in which we see ourselves and our world directly influences the reality we experience*. Fortunately, the illusion of ourselves as apart from the rest of reality is disappearing before our eyes. As we "look out" at life, we see only ourselves facing a mirror. All that we see is that which we are. There is no separation. We may now choose to hold in mind a comprehensive vision that includes everything—all that we see through our normal vision, all that we can perceive through alternate modes of consciousness, and all that exists only in the realm of possibility.

Rumor has it that the reason we are beginning to see so many UFOs is not because they have just arrived, but rather because our eyes are opening. The UFOs have always been there, but we have been unable to see them. As our awareness attunes to subtler vibratory patterns, UFO configurations become more apparent. Who knows what else we may see as our eyes continue to open.

We are awakening. We can be responsible. We can begin to view ourselves as part of the long magical process of evolution.

Humanity is a great experiment of Divine
intention, an adventure in transforma-
tion, a seeking, a reaching forward, an
exploration into the unknown.

We are asked to partkae in this play—consciously and joyfully.

Cancer and Evolution

As far as we know the Gaian self-regulative intelligence is doing just fine in maintaining harmony and permitting conditions for subsequent evolution. In spite of the many pollutants that humans place in the biosphere, Gaia has demonstrated a great variety of defense mechanisms that help her to cope with our toxic influences. There is one problem, however—the cancerous growth of Humanity.

Cancer can be described as a cellular growth that is relatively independent of and indifferent to the wellbeing of the body. Originally these cells have their appropriate function. Sometimes, however, things get out of hand and this unruly group grows and expands without concern for the health of the larger whole. Unchecked self-interest, without regard for the rest of the system, seems to be the problem.

Although we have come to partial solutions in dealing with cancer, we have not as yet discovered its basic cause nor even less its possible potential. Perhaps it is a mutant evolutionary energy that is waiting to be appropriately expressed. When it does not find a creative outlet it goes on growing within the organism, with destructive results. Perhaps there is a hidden evolutionary potential.

In some individuals a spontaneous remission from cancer has been observed—often preceded or accompanied by a profound insight or a new sense of meaning. Could it be that the cancerous energy was brought back to its higher potential and used as a channel for a source of inspiration? We simply do not know.

One of the most innovative and effective means of arresting cancer has been through the use of visualization. Inwardly imagining the cancerous energy field returning to its right relationship within :he organism seems to turn the tide. Inwardly viewing the psychophyiscal self in a vibrant healthy condition calls forth a return to health.

If we now look again at Humanity as a cancerous tissue in the body of Gaia, it is evident that we have multiplied promiscuously! We have behaved in our own self-interest with little regard for the whole, and we have failed to understand, much less participate in, the essential function of the Earth. We are still doing "our own thing" and wondering why we experience so much confusion.

Perhaps as we become more self-conscious we will check our cancerous growth. Perhaps as we begin to visualize ourselves in right relation to a vibrant healthy planetary being, we will help in the healing, we will call forth and co-create a state of planetary wholeness.

The School of Evolution

Each of us begins at square one, focusing on physical health, psychological wellbeing and spiritual attunement as preparation for conscious evolutionary service.

> We are now too close to each other for the old kind of individualism to be bearable. The interaction is too powerful. What is in front of us is the need for change to an attitude in which we accept that every man has to serve a cosmic purpose. . .
>
> (Bennett, 1977:50)

There are stepping stones however—lessons to be learned along the way. In the progression from self-centeredness to cosmic identity, there are many programs in the school of conscious evolution. Life's curriculum offers a variety of courses, such as the couple relationship, group and community, land trusts, bioregional social organization and planetary stewardship.

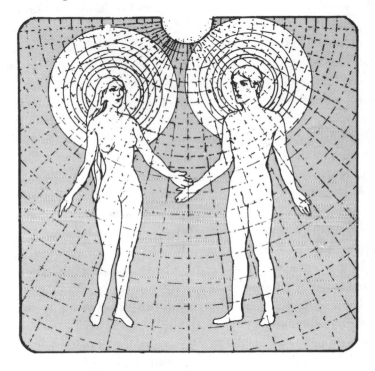

Beyond the individual, the next step toward collective consciousness is the couple. As a result of commitment, work and a sense of playfulness, it is possible for two people to embark on *The Couple's Journey* (Campbell, 1980), to pass through a series of developmental stages and to approach a direct experience of transpersonal consciousness. This involves both partners seeking a balance of masculine (active) and feminine (receptive) qualities within themselves. This involves each person finding a deep sense of personal and spiritual identity. In this way a true marriage can occur in which two strong beings are united to become one.

Examples of the potency of combined "synergized" energies of the couple are found in every field of human activity: Marie and Pierre Currie in science; Eleanor and Franklin Roosevelt in government; Yoko Ono and John Lennon in entertainment; Eileen and Peter Caddy, founders of the Findhorn Community in Scotland.

The next challenge is that of group consciousness. This is quite the opposite of mass phenomena, which is entirely unconscious. The study of group consciousness requires ongoing attention and awareness, not only of oneself, but also of one's relationship with others and with the group as a whole. Such a task is nearly impossible, yet absolutely necessary. In order that this experiment in conscious evolution be effective, it is necessary that group members hold a larger aim in focus and judge the group's failures and accomplishments in relation to it. As the group evolves, differentiation will occur as specific members demonstrate unique talents and interests. Also, a nuclear subgroup of individuals will appear to serve the leadership function. Such a role, however, in a group committed to evolutionary service can only be taken properly when the leadership function is informed and directed by an inner source of guidance.

Groups and communities in all parts of the planet are experimenting with new ways of living and working together. The Farm in Tennessee experiments with simple living and social service as guiding principles. The Findhorn Community, in Northern Scotland, informed by guidance from the devic and spiritual realms, offers educational programs in the arts of planetary transformation. Auroville in India translates the vision of Sri Aurobindo into an experimental city designed to express a more conscious way of life. The Institute for the Study of Conscious Evolution in San Francisco (see Appendix A) brings together diverse spiritual perspectives into research work focused on the discovery of new values and behaviors that will bring us—Humanity—into harmonious relationship with one another and with the Earth. In addition, a number of governmental and business organizations are now operating from a broad perspective that takes into account both individual and global needs. Such experiments are many—the possibilities unlimited.

As we in the Western technological culture move toward a more balanced relationship with Gaia we notice that we have forgotten something essential. We have forgotten our job of caring for Mother Earth. Some traditional native peoples, however, still retain this knowledge. Certain indigenous groups such as the Hopi feel it is their sacred duty to protect and care for the lands they inhabit. No one owns the land—for it is owned by the Great Spirit. The land therefore is a gift to humankind, offered in sacred trust.

In our culture the land trust is a relatively new concept in land ownership and management that recalls us to our sacred function. Land, purchased or contributed, is placed in public trust with specific covenants that thereafter determine its use. These guidelines generally reflect consideration for the Earth and its ecosystems, including the right balance of human involvement.

A group or community who agree to live in harmony with the land may assume stewardship and remain as stewards as long as they comply with the convenants. In this way the land trust/ stewardship contract ensures a continuing right relationship— free from private interests—between Humanity and Mother Earth.

Beyond the stewardship role that a specific group may assume, a larger level of social experiment is emerging. The focus is on bioregional community development. This is in a sense a return to an ancient way of life in which communities

coordinate their activities in relation to the available resources
and ecological needs of a specific geological region.

   The bioregion is a natural unity bound together by environmental factors, such as watershed, climatic integrity (desert) or
terrain (coastal or mountain). Through intentional consideration of the eco-dynamics of a specific region, the environment
is preserved and enhanced. Such clustering of community focus
may one day in the future replace national boundaries that
have been unconsciously set (as a result of war for example)
without regard for natural bioregional integrity.

These and many other social and environmental experiments point toward a conscious alignment with and service to the needs of the Earth. In this way we work toward assuming our rightful role of planetary stewardship.

The Creative Unknown
It is clear that the vision and possibilities outlined in this book are extremely ambitious. But perhaps we have no choice; perhaps the only way to go is forward.

> The truth is that as one's real power grows and his knowledge widens, ever the way he can follow grows narrower until at last he chooses nothing but does only and wholly what he must do.
>
> (LeGuin, 1975:37)

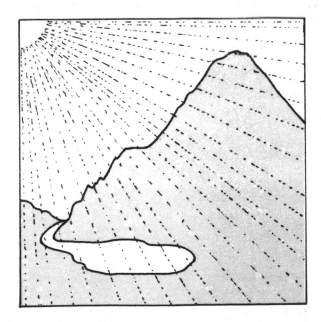

And yet although there is only one way, there are no specific guidelines, no predetermined maps for the journey. We move into unchartered territory; we unfold the creative unknown.

The past need not be our program. Our suffering is of the past; our joy will be discovered in our evolutionary future. If we go against the natural force of evolution, we will exhaust ourselves. As we move with it, we will find ourselves empowered and enlightened.

What we choose to create will lead us to our destiny. Divine intention is available to help—not to demand or determine. We have been made in the image of God to behave like gods. The challenge before us is to embody divine qualities such as wisdom, patience, love and compassion. The challenge is to manifest these qualities in our life on Earth.

 We have in our bodies, hearts, minds and spirits the wisdom of the ages. We have at our fingertips all the wonders of modern technology. We have the East and the West, the yin and the yang—infused, informed and guided by the brilliant intention of evolution. The time is here to envision and co-create the adventure of conscious evolution.

Afterword

by

Virginia Satir

I thought Virginia Satir would be a good
person to ask for an Afterword, for although
Virginia is a world traveler and renowned
speaker, she is also one of the most down-to-
earth people I know. So I invited her to help
make a transition from my world of theory and
principles to the realm of everyday life, to the
world in which we touch and feel, laugh and
cry, work, play and make love.
She did not disappoint me—her comments deal,
on the one hand, with life as it is and with
practical next steps. At the same time, she
expressed a remarkably deep confidence in
people—a sense that we are just beginning to
tap the vast reservoir of human potential.

(Author's note)

The ideas expressed in *Conscious Evolution* are broad and
sweeping. I would like to express some thoughts simply, and
suggest how we can begin to work with them. First of all,
conscious evolution means that one can do things in front of
one's eyes instead of behind one's back. One can direct change
consciously. Secondly it means seeking a new model of what
the human being can be—a model based on growth and expansion rather than on limitation and deprivation. Historically,
we've never had a model of what a human being can be. Our
prevailing model has been of what one should be or shouldn't
be. Maybe, now in the nineteen hundred eighties, we can leave
that one and look for the possibilities inherent in being human.

I no longer ask myself the question whether anyone can grow since I know they can, the question is *when* and *how;* what are the limits, if any; what are the new possibilities? This becomes exciting.

Up to now we've been working with a model of what's wrong —pathology, evil, and problems—so that all of our thinking has been geared towards how to get rid of illness. We are just coming into what it means to be a well person, a happy person. I have a strong feeling that I don't have to do very much with problems, if I work toward developing health. As a consequence "problems" are no longer necessary. The elements of health and the elements of illness are not the same. When one gets a hole in one's plumbing, one doesn't learn how to repair it by only studying how it happened. The new thing now for me, and I guess for the world, is the breakthrough into what creates wellness. I'll give you an example.

Up until the middle fifties, everyone thought that after one got to be sixty or so one ought to be senile—because that's the way a human being was. Those ideas came from people who were sick. When we started studying the well people who were seventy, eighty and one hundred, we discovered new possibilities that had neither been tapped nor understood.

Another special area that needs attention is "work." Many people have lived for work because work meant money, and money meant prestige, apart from the basic survival needs. I think work is important. It is a vehicle for expressing ourselves and for participating and contributing. However, many people are out there doing boring things, "enduring" their life at work, and frequently missing the entire joyful process of life.

Let's take a look at this survival that so many people are seeking. First, there's survival of the body, but then there's the survival of the spirit and soul. Learning how to survive joyfully has had little attention. I often wonder what the world would look like if people did work so that they were fully expressing themselves, so that they were excited and challenged, as well as contributing. Within that frame of thinking, fewer people would work on the assembly lines for long periods of time because when the challenge wore off, it would become boring. They would feel their neurological system becoming stultified as the senses stopped reacting. They would want more.

One of the things I do is help people to make work a piece of their expression. Since we live in a money culture, money needs to be involved. But money can become something different, something that can be used as a tool for further expression instead of being used as a vehicle of enslavement. I think we've been going at it "backwards."

Healthy change hinges on people taking responsibility for themselves. I met a man the other day, a high government official who had been in a poor area in South Africa. He asked the people there, "What can we do to be most helpful to you?" The answer came back, "Educate yourself; educate your own people." What that meant was, "Get your house in order and do what you can to really make your own self grow." That's the first step.

It's so easy to go around doing things for other people before you've done something for yourself. For instance, finding out how to live your life without blaming other people; finding out how to discover the creativeness within yourself, to stand on your own feet, to take your own responsibility for your participation. We're far away from that, and our laws and our institutions are also far away from that. My hunch is that the next steps are to increase our capacity to be non-judgmental and to simultaneously discover new and exciting aspects of people. This will go a long way toward creating new possibilities for people in our institutions.

Most of Western Culture has embraced a linear approach which essentially emphasizes logic and analysis. Softness and roundness are considered weak. What we now need are models that show what I call *seed power*, which includes both softness and hardness. We need desperately to realize there is nothing weak about roundness, softness and gentleness.

Our world has been run mostly on what we call yang, or male energy. As long as we have only that, we have to have wars and all the other destructive things that are going on.

There's an old fable in which the sun and wind have a fight about who is the most powerful. Just then they see a man walking on the earth. So they say to each other, "Well, let's see who is the most powerful. Let's see who can get his coat first." The wind blew and blew and blew, and all the man did was to move his coat around himself tighter and tighter. Then the sun gently came out and brought warmth. The man immediately took off his coat because he was too hot. This is the kind of power I'm speaking about. The inclusion of the yin, or female energy, is essential. In a sense we have all been going around half-wits, because we have not added this piece. We need to become "whole-wits." We need to include the male and the female parts, present in each of us; we need to include more of this "seed and sun power."

This imbalance is reflected in our personal relationships. Love is often perceived as a bargaining table, a substitute for somebody's own responsibilities. "If you love me, then you'll take care of me." I think love is a feeling that comes about as a natural thing. Love is an experience of an integration with the soul. It doesn't have a price tag on it. It's a condition of radiance and joy. This is what makes it possible for the atmosphere to be alive. This means that it's necessary for each person to have the freedom to let go, the freedom to know that they don't own anybody except themselves. Relationships then can be described with a small "my" rather than a big capital "MY."

As a person begins to be able to differentiate and take responsibility, a real self-integration can occur. This is a place of freedom. From here, the ability to love is not weak; it is powerful.

As we begin to connect with our personal power, we can connect with an even deeper source. There is within each of us a "wise one." The "wise one" is one of these beings that will not do anything unless asked. The "wise one" doesn't make uninvited appearances, doesn't intrude unless one is ready. When one is consumed by anxieties about living, the "wise one" stays asleep. That's why meditation is so helpful. Through meditation the "wise one" is right there to say: "Oh, goody, goody, I've got a chance now." The "wise one" is waiting, as it were, for an invitation. When I introduce people to their "wise one," they're always astounded at how much they know. Because their "wise one" knows everything. It's all right there. It's truly amazing.

It's a fact that we have a fantastic brain that has only been touched by, probably, say two percent of its potential. We have wonderful capacities in ourselves. The human organism is capable of fantastic things, but we know little about it because we've been looking at this miracle in little pieces—the brain over there, the heart over there, the soul over there, etc. The poor thing has become stretched apart. However, things are beginning to change. People are beginning to see things differently. They are beginning to be more conscious of what they are about and what is possible for them.

The difficulty with the idea of conscious evolution is that it is a noun. It has to become a verb. It has to be something that's in process, that's actually occurring.

Based upon what we know human beings are like, we see that we now actually can begin *to consciously evolve*. That means "I'm paying attention, I'm giving attention, I'm conscious." Life is not only going on behind my back; it's also going on in front of my eyes. It's the difference between having the reins on your shoulder with somebody driving you from the back and having the reins in your hands with you driving.

We've been "driven" for thousands of years. Now it's time for us to begin to do our own driving; to be what we really can be

—full of radiance and love, as well as effectiveness and compe-
tence. For me conscious evolution means taking the next step
toward being fully human.

Glossary of Evolutionary Terms

Absolute: The ultimate source of creation; the highest, most profound Being in which all else finds its relative being.

active will: The expression of will in which the individual's personal understanding and potency are foreground in determining and initiating an action (see *will* and *receptive will*).

alchemy: The art of transmuting coarse or dense psychic energies into finer energies; the seemingly miraculous process of self-transformation to deeper levels of consciousness.

attention: The capacity to focus or concentrate on something. Attention can be developed first through focusing on the immediate sense of one's being and then expanded to embrace deeper and more inclusive levels of being.

awaken: To become increasingly aware of one's presence and of one's immediate and cosmic context.

bioregion: A specific geographic area having some degree of environmental integrity, therefore requiring consideration as an integrated eco-system that places definite constraints on land and resource development.

biosphere: All the land, water and air of planet Earth inhabited by life; the home of Gaia's sensitive, self-regulative intelligence.

Bodhisattva: The mythic being (in Buddhist tradition) or quality that chooses service to all sentient beings before personal release from suffering.

channeling: The process by which a person or group receives information or guidance from a higher or transpersonal source of intelligence.

co-creation: The creative process in which individuals cooperate with one another or with a source of inner, higher intention in bringing something into being.

conscience: An inherent inclination to do that which is good or right, specifically, that which serves the evolution of self, Humanity, the Earth and the Universe.

143

consciousness: The state of being directly aware of one's self as a living being and as an aspect of a living Universe. Degree of consciousness varies from moment to moment. An increase in mean level leads to an increase in capacity to participate in conscious evolution.

conscious evolution: Volitional participation in the process of evolution, especially in cooperation with an inner intention of transpersonal origin. (See expanded definition opposite Table of Contents.)

cosmic force: A subtle, non-material influence that affects terrestrial conditions, often in "mysterious" ways.

critical mass: That proportion of change in any system that stimulates (magically) that change in the entire system.

Divine Will: The creative intention from which springs all life. The source of evolutionary pattern and process.

ecosystem: Any interdependent community of parts that inter-relate in a balanced, holistic way and thereby provide for the harmony, wellbeing and perpetuity of the whole system.

egoism: A separative tendency that places self-interest before all else; the doctrine that self-interest is the proper goal of all human actions.

entropy: A process of increasing disorder and decreasing available energy. Taken alone, this process implies the absence of creative evolutionary intention.

esoteric: Hidden from view, especially from our ordinary mode of discriminative perception.

esoteric group: A group of individuals who study and work together: in order to change themselves toward alternate modes of perception and higher levels of being; and in order to assume a specific role in relation to the process of conscious evolution.

essence: The intrinsic, fundamental nature of one's being; that which exists a priori to all that is learned in this life.

ETA: Evolutionary transformative agent—the agent within any organism (person, society, or planet) that initiates self-transcendent change and growth.

etheric: Of a subtle, non-material nature, usually imbued with spiritual qualities.

free energy: Released energy that has not been assigned a specific homeostatic function; potential force that has become available for new creative work.

Gaia: Mother Earth, the planet perceived as a living intelligent being.

genetic lineage: The specific body of information that is transmitted by the DNA through the generations of a species; that which programs cow to be calf to be cow, etc.

geomancy: The art of devining and channeling subtle currents of energy that flow on the Earth; the study of the Earth as a living energy system.

guidance: Instructive information received from an inner, spiritual source of intelligence.

harmonization: Bringing the parts of any organism or organization into cooperative, integrated relationship.

holistic: Recognizing the interdependence and integrity of all parts and processes of any system; ultimately only the Universe can be fully regarded as a holistic entity.

holography: The study of interference patterns and reconstituted images leading to the hypothesis that all manifest reality can be regarded as interference patterns in the flow and interplay of energy fields.

homeostasis: A stable state of equilibrium between the parts or subsystems of any organism.

homocentric: The worldview that places human interests before all else, especially before the interests of other terrestrial species and kingdoms; of Gaia, herself; and of beings from other places, spaces and dimensions.

Human Being: The collective being comprised of all individual humans; the potential psychic entity that has the capacity to serve a specific function in relation to Gaia.

intuition: The immediate apprehension of something without the use of rational thought; a direct knowing derived from a hidden, inner source of understanding.

land stewardship: A sacred trust assumed by an individual or group who agree to honor, nurture and live in harmony with a specific tract of land.

land trust: A concept or legal agreement that places a piece of land in public trust with specific convenants that thereafter determine its use. These guidelines generally reflect a primary consideration for the Earth and its ecosystems, including a right balance of human involvement.

metaprinciple: A principle that embodies and implies the unitive, integrative nature of the Universe.

metascience: A potential science that integrates intuitive, spiritual understanding with rational, empirical enquiry; a science that holds a priori the fundamental integrity of the Universe.

multidimensional: Consisting of various dimensions or levels of being, one contained within the next in a mutually inclusive system.

New Age: The vision that Humanity and Earth are entering an era of peace, harmony and mutual understanding that will be infused with and informed by spiritual guidance.

noosphere: The thinking layer of the biosphere, composed of the collective mental energies of humankind.

objective reality: That which exists a priori to human perception.

ontogony: The life cycle of a single orgamism.

perception: The act of knowing or interpreting the world around us. Perception varies greatly according to background, state of consciousness and intention.

personal: Pertaining to an individual, especially those aspects of the person that are uniquely individual and not of a transpersonal nature (see *transpersonal*).

personality: The acquired or learned qualities and behavioral patterns of an individual: distinguished from essential qualities.

phylogeny: The evolutionary development of a species or race over long periods of time.

planetary consciousness: The mind or intelligence of Gaia in which the collective human consciousness may play a role.

planetary function: The specific role that any part or process may play in the drama of planetary evolution.

Planetary Logos: The sacred mind and being of a planet, specifically of planet Earth viewed as a participant in cosmic evolution.

planetary stewardship: The sacred function of Humanity to protect, conserve and enhance the environment and consciousness of Gaia.

principle: A natural underlying tendency or process that manifests in various phenomena.

projection: The process by which ideas or images are ascribed to persons or objects other than oneself. This process, usually unconscious, can become conscious and can potentially play a helpful role in conscious evolution.

psyche: The mind; the system of subtle energies that makes up the non-material totality of a person. The individual psyche is intimately wed with transpersonal dimensions of the collective Psyche.

psychic: Of or referring to the psyche; of the subtler levels of human understanding and action.

purpose: The end toward which one aims, specifically the raison d'etre of an individual or group in relation to the work of conscious evolution.

quantum: An indivisible entity or unit, progression beyond which requires a leap to another discrete level.

ray of creation: A strand of manifestation emanating from the Absolute down into dense matter. Earth finds itself toward the lower end of one such ray (see Ouspensky, 1949).

receptive will: The expression of will in which an individual chooses to transmit, be influenced by and serve an intention coming from a transpersonal source of guidance (see *will* and *active will*).

resonance: An effect created when the vibratory quality of the parts come into harmonic relationship with the whole; when this occurs the capacities of the whole are magnified.

right-relationship: A quality of relationship between individual parts or between the parts and the whole in which all are nourished and encouraged toward self-development and mutual harmonious integration.

sacred space: A special place within the individual or within the world wherein the energy field permits, even enhances, the possibility for experiencing the sacred. People go to a sacred space for renewal, inspiration and vision.

Self: The spiritual center from which our individual selves are born, from which we receive guidance and inspiration.

self-consciousness: An intermediate stage en route to a full Self-realization wherein the individual becomes aware of living-presence in the moment and aware of the forces that are motivating personal choice and action.

separative: Placing oneself or one's interest before consideration of the context in which one lives.

service: The act of giving of oneself to providing for the needs of the whole. In this age service to the planet Earth is called for. Good news—service to the whole provides abundantly for the fulfillment of the part.

spiritual: Pertaining to those transpersonal dimensions of consciousness in which we find the experience of unity. When we touch the spiritual, we know we have come home at last.

Solar Logos: The sacred mind and spirit of The Solar Being, centered in the Sun, extending to the limits of the solar system and in dialogue with other heavenly beings.

subpersonalities: Aspects of the personality that are distinct in their interests and aims. Discrete jumps of identity occur as new situations present themselves and trigger different subpersonalities.

subjective reality: That which exists as a result of human perception, hence *everything we know* (except in very rare moments of objective clarity).

syntropy: A process of increasing order, energy, harmony and consciousness. This process implies recognition of creative evolutionary intention.

thoughtform: Any idea or concept that is held in individual or group mind with adequate intensity to permit the integration of a coherent energy pattern. Powerful thoughtforms have the capacity to influence the beliefs, thoughts and actions of Humanity.

tradition: An ancient lineage of beliefs, customs, rituals and teachings, especially with regard to knowledge of spiritual practices and perspectives.

transformation: To change the condition, function or nature of, especially in relation to individual and planetary evolution.

transmission: A passing through of deep wisdom; reception and expression of guidance.

transpersonal: Referring to those dimensions of being or consciousness wherein individuals share a common identity; those dimensions wherein we are one. (Understanding this definition may require experiential background.)

unitive: Consideration of the needs of the whole simultaneous with consideration of personal needs.

will: The potential power for choice, decision or action—varies extremely according to person and circumstance (see *active will* and *receptive will*).

References and Resources

Anonymous (1908). *Kaballion.* Yogi Publication Society, Chicago.

Anonymous (1975). *The Rainbow Bridge.* New Age Press, Los Angeles.

Assagiolio, Roberto (1965). *Psychosynthesis.* The Viking Press, New York.

Aurobindo, Sri (1974). *The Future Evolution of Man.* The Theosophical Publishing House, Wheaton, Ill.

Aurobindo, Sri (1977). *The Life Divine.* Sri Aurobindo Ashram Trust, Pondicherry, India.

Bailey, Alice A. (1962). *A Treatise on Cosmic Fire.* Lucis Publishing Co., New York.

Bailey, Alice A. (1970). *Esoteric Psychology.* Lucis Publishing Co., New York.

Bennett, John G. (1973). *Needs of a New Age Community.* Coombe Springs Press, Gloucestershire, England.

Blair, Lawrence (1975). *Rhythms of Vision.* Warner Books, New York.

Blavatsky, H. P. (1952). *The Secret Doctrine.* Theosophical University Press, Pasadena, Ca.

Campbell, Susan (1980). *The Couple's Journey.* Impact Publishers, San Luis Obispo, Ca.

Capra, Fritjof (1975). *The Tao of Physics.* Shambala Publications, Inc., Boulder, Colo.

Charpentier, Louis (1972). *The Chartres Cathedral.* Research into Lost Knowledge Organization, London.

Chaudhuri, Haridas (1977). "Asian Psychology." Barry McWaters (ed.), *Humanistic Perspectives.* Brooks Cole Publishing Co., Monterey, Ca.

Dobzhanski, Theodosius, et al (1977). *Evolution.* W.H. Freeman & Co., San Francisco.

Ferguson, Marilyn (1979). *The Aquarian Conspiracy.* J.P. Tarcher, Los Angeles.

Fortune, Dion (1974). *Esoteric Philosophy of Love and Marriage.* Samuel Weiser, Inc., New York.

Fuller, Buckminster (1963). *No More Secondhand God.* Southern Illinois University Press, Carbondale, Ill.

Gribbin, John (1971). *Our Changing Planet.* Thomas Y. Crowell Co., New York.

Gurdjieff, G.I. (1964). *All and Everything.* E.P. Dutton Co., New York.

Gurdjieff, G.I. (1969). *Meetins with Remarkable Men.* E.P. Dutton Co., New York.

Hubbard, Barbara Marx (1978). *Evolutionary Journal.* Futures Network, Washington, D.C.

Jung, C.G. (1971). *The Portable Jung;* Campbell, Joseph, (ed.) The Viking Press, New York.

LeGuin, Ursula (1975). *A Wizard of Earthsea.* Bantam Books, New York.

LeShan, Lawrence (1969). "Physicists and Mystics: Similarities in World View." *Journal of Transpersonal Psychology,* Fall 1969, Vol. 1, No. 2, pp. 1-20.

Lovelock, James and Epton, Sidney (1975). "The Quest for Gaia." *The New Scientist,* 6 February 1975, pp. 304-306.

Marguelles, Lynn (1970). *The Origin of the Eucaryotic Cell.* Yale University Press, New Haven.

McWaters, Barry (ed.) (1977). *Humanistic Perspectives.* Brooks Cole Publishers, Monterey, Ca.

Mehta, Rohit (1961). *The Eternal Light.* Theosophical Publishing House, Adyar, India.

Michell, John (1969). *The View Over Atlantis.* Ballantine Books, New York.

Miller, James Grier (1978). *Living Systems.* McGraw-Hill Book Co., New York.

Needleman, Jacob (1980). *Lost Christianity.* Doubleday, New York.

Ouspensky, P.D. (1949). *In Search of the Miraculous.* Harcourt, Brace & World, Inc., New York.

Plato (1945). *The Republic;* Concord, Francis Macdonald, (tr.) Oxford University Press, New York.

Powell, Arthur E. (1930). *The Solar System.* Theosophical Publishing House Ltd., London.

de Puruker, G. (1977). *Man in Evolution.* Theosophical Pubversity, Adyar, India.

Rama, Swami, et al (1976). *Yoga and Psychotherapy.* Himalayan Institute, Glenview, Ill.

Satprem (1974). *Sri Aurobindo, or The Adventure of Consciousness.* Harper & Row, New York.

Schaya, Leo (1973). *The Universal Meaning of the Kabbalah.* Penguin Books, Baltimore.

Shah, Idris (1971). *The Sufis.* Doubleday, New York.

Spangler, David (1971). *Links with Space.* Findhorn Foundation, Forres, Scotland.

Spangler, David (1976). *Revelation.* The Rainbow Bridge, San Francisco.

Spangler, David (1977). *Toward a Planetary Vision.* Findhorn Foundation, Forres, Scotland.

Steiner, Rudolf (1970). *At the Gates of Spiritual Science.* Rudolf Steiner Press, London.

Svent-Gyoergi, Albert (1974). "Drive in Living Matter to Perfect Itself." *Synthesis,* Vol. I, No. 1, pp. 12-24.

Teilhard de Chardin, Pierre (1961). *The Phenomenon of Man.* Harper & Row, New York.

Thomas, Lewis (1975). *The Lives of a Cell.* Bantam Books, New York.

Whyte, Lancelot Law (1965). *Internal Factors in Evolution.* Braziller, New York.

Young, Arthur (1976). *The Reflexive Universe.* Delacorte Press, San Francisco.

Yutang, Lin (ed.) (1955). *The Wisdom of China and India.* The Modern Library, New York.

Zink, David (1978). *The Stones of Atlantis.* Prentice Hall Inc., Englewood Cliffs, N.J.

Zukav, Gary (1979). *The Dancing Wu Li Masters.* William Morrow & Co., Inc., New York.

Appendix A

The Institute for the Study of Conscious Evolution

A Brief Prospectus

The Institute for the Study of Conscious Evolution (ISCE) was founded in 1977 as a non-profit, tax-exempt research and educational organization. The guiding purpose is to foster responsible, conscious participation in individual, human and planetary evolution, i.e., to find practical ways to work together toward creating a realistic, positive future. Since its founding ISCE has sponsored many public service and educational programs. Currently eight projects are active, each focusing on a different aspect of the overall work of conscious evolution. Projects are staffed by researchers from a variety of disciplines and world views, working collaboratively to develop methods of inquiry, education, and social action.

ISCE is committed to "hold in mind" a positive vision of the future—a vision in which there is equal emphasis on individual self-realization and cooperative social harmony. From an evolutionary, planetary perspective, ISCE has initiated specific work to:

- provide a context for interdisciplinary inquiry and research
- develop alternate research models
- initiate group inquiry and research in evolutionary psychology; education; man/woman and family relationships; governance in group life; community development; networking; ecology; alternate energy resources; and planetary ecosystems.
- offer consultation to corporate executives and organizational development practitioners
- train professional and pre-professional psychologists and family counselors

- sponsor lectures and workshops for the public
- offer weekly learning groups
- prepare a quarterly publication, entitled *GAIA*, to report our work and related research

In summary, ISCE is working toward a balanced manifestation of three inseparable, interdependent qualities of conscious evolution—individual wellbeing, social harmony and human/ environmental right relationship.

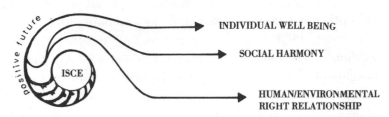

Need and Purpose

It has become increasingly clear to all who are concerned that we—Humanity—can no longer assume that the human species and its institutions will continue to spontaneously evolve in a positive way. The forces that have molded us thus far are no longer adequate. If we depend on them alone, we are surely in grave trouble.

Our most advanced thinkers posit that we are entering an era wherein cooperative participation and responsibility are not only ideal, but mandatory. In order to prepare for such involvement, we must be willing to awaken and actualize our potentials for enlightened consciousness and for cooperative action in the service of the whole—qualities which enable individuals to find direction and meaning in life. Deep and comprehensive study is needed to inform our consciousness. Enlightened action is required to take the next steps toward a cooperative future. ISCE has come into being in order to respond to these challenges.

In what ways is it possible for Humanity, intentionally and consciously, to participate in the survival and evolution of the species and the planet? How to join in the work and adventure of conscious evolution?

The purpose of ISCE is to synthesize *inner search, outer research, education,* and *service* in a design that enables practical responses to the above questions. These responses draw upon the interfacing frontiers of a variety of disciplines— the physical, natural and social sciences, philosophy, art, religion, etc. Further, the Institute provides a context for the synthesis of East and West, intuition and rationality, global perception and analytic thought, being and doing, etc.

In short, ISCE works toward bringing together the deep wisdom of the ancient spiritual traditions with the brilliant insights of contemporary science. In this way we support the emergence of a synthesis that will enable the birth of a new age of personal and social harmony.

World Needs/ISCE Responses

Viewing our planet as one interdependent system, we see a number of areas of acute need.

Need Indicators

1. Survival—epidemic disease and starvation
2. Social—war, crime and unemployment
3. Ecological—environmental pollution and resource depletion
4. Psychological—mental dysfunctions and daily stress
5. Spiritual—pervasive sense of lack or ennui

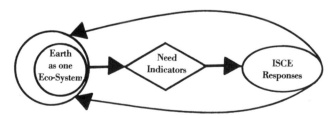

Dedicated to an interdisciplinary, multi-faceted approach to these needs, ISCE is committed to at least two levels of response to each need area: 1) Theory (T) and model building, which can help us to re-image and re-form ourselves and our reality toward a better future; and 2) Practice (P) which initiates proactive responses to specific issues that call for direct action. Samples of current responses follow:

ISCE Response: Theory (T) and Practice (P)

1. Survival

   (T): Clarify and communicate the meaning of human interdependence to show how the distress or wellbeing of each part of the larger organism (Humanity) affects all other parts.

   (P): Sponsor fundraising events for specific causes, such as Cambodian relief and Hopi land preservation.

2. Social

   (T): Create models of positive community, organizational development and effective governance processes.

   (P): Develop a farm/eco-community in which individuals can live and work in harmony with the Earth.

3. Ecological

   (T): Design models and educational programs in human/environment "right relationship." Discover actual human/planetary energy field interactions.

   (P): Develop alternative energy resources. Raise funds and initiate research to support preservation of sites of special religious and geopsychic significance.

4. Psychological

   (T): Develop overview of a comprehensive "psychology of conscious evolution" and a related methodology for individual and group change.

   (P): Train para-professional and professional counselors to work with principles and tools of evolutionary psychology—emphasizing the discovery of meaning and purpose in life. Offer talk and dialogue series on topics related to evolution of consciousness.

5. Spiritual

(T): Construct a vision or model of individual consciousness as a creative aspect of larger, transpersonal fields of
consciousness.

(P): Offer groups for learning meditative practice and
for generating resonant energy fields.

Systems Overview

Another depiction of the Institute's orientation is expressed in
the following "systems" model. Information is received both
from within via *inner search* (meditation, intuition, psychic
attunement, etc.) and from without via observation and
analytic research; processed by the Institute groups; and re-
expressed to the world via *evolutionary education* programs
and *practical service* projects.

This comprehensive approach—including both inner and
outer sources of information and work for world change on
both theoretical and practical levels—is one of the unique
characteristics of ISCE. Hence, one of our general goals is to
remain true to this balanced orientation.

These four components—*inner search, analytic research,
evolutionary education* and *practical service*—are expressed
more fully in the following diagram and definitions.

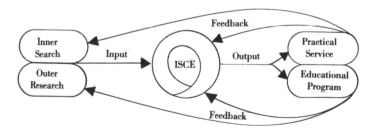

Inner Search

- to seek guidance for our work from inner transpersonal
sources of wisdom;

- to provide a context for personal search toward a deepened, more inclusive sense of identity;
- To develop, through group meditation practice, a spiritually attuned, resonant energy field within which our work has optimum support;
- to seek and discover through experiential, comparative study the common elements among a variety of spiritual and psychological paths of consciousness exploration;

Analytic Research
- to develop research questions and hypotheses leading toward specific findings;
- to observe phenomena and accurately measure and record data;
- to systematically analyze the data and to draw relevant conclusions;
- to discover and practice new modes of inquiry which view the phenomena being studied in holistic relationship to their context.

Evolutionary Education
- to disseminate, to the membership and the public, information aimed at assisting individuals and groups to refine and focus their efforts to live in harmony with the principles of conscious evolution;
- to offer this information through a variety of forms including publications, films, tapes, lectures, seminars, ongoing courses of study, radio and television programs, etc.

Practical Service
- to identify areas of need and to administer programs which directly respond to these needs, with particular emphasis on enhancing capacities for self-healing and renewal.

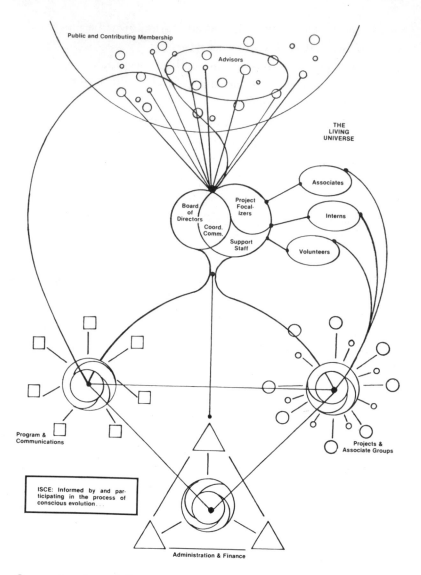

Organizational Overview

Any visual overview of ISCE organization and process ideally includes a sense of movement, of communication flow, and of interpenetration of responsibilities. As each participant holds the vision of the whole, while simultaneously allowing that vision to transform itself, the organization begins to appear as a multi-dimensional mobile sculpture, characterized by the rhythms of a living organism.

Current Work and Projects

ISCE's research, education and service work are accomplished through several vehicles:

Research Projects—eight projects provide a context for Associates from a variety of disciplines to work in teams, focusing on a specific aspect of evolutionary work, ranging from research in earth energies to the creation of new models of organizational management.

Associate Groups—offer weekly ongoing personal and professional development experiences for ISCE Associates in ways designed to foster integration of personal growth and planetary service.

Public Programs and Communications—ISCE sponsors a variety of programs aimed at familiarizing the public with ways they can foster conscious evolution in their daily lives and work.

A Final Note

The comprehensive, planetary focus of ISCE offers a potentially unifying theme around which a great variety of disciplines and perspectives can find a common sense of purpose— and, ultimately, a common work toward the wellbeing of the whole. This planetary emphasis not only has the potential for helping to integrate the efforts of various disciplines and interest groups, but can also lead to the development of a new model of inquiry. This model is based on a recognition of the inseparability of inner meditative search and outer analytic research—of both values and action.

The interdisciplinary work of the Institute is intended to enhance individual consciousness and health, social harmony and human/planetary right relationship. By virtue of this holistic approach, we hope and believe that ISCE will make a unique contribution to the future.

Those seeking further information or wishing to receive GAIA, ISCE's quarterly publication, may write to the Institute for the Study of Conscious Evolution, 2418 Clement St., San Francisco, California 94121.

Appendix B

Dimensions of Conscious Evolution

by Barry McWaters, Ph.D.

What role can the individual play in the larger processes of human and cosmic evolution? In this paper I propose that the very activity of individual search for transpersonal realization plays a significant role in evolution. As more and more individuals gain a deeper sense of self and a deeper realization of the profound unity of all that exists, Humanity, as a potential living being, becomes more self-conscious, more internally harmonious and ultimately more functional in the evolutionary process of the cosmos.

In order to explore this perspective more fully, two complementary yet distinct, transformational processes are examined —"transformation of being" and "transformation of form." Both have been described as evolution. By studying these processes in conjunction, a more clear understanding of our potential for conscious evolution becomes possible.

Transformation of Being
Figure 1: The Vertical Dimension

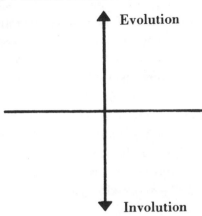

163

The term transformation generally describes a change of some sort in a positive or growthful direction. Within the field of Transpersonal Psychology this term, for the most part, has referred to the potential expansion of individual consciousness or being. This transformational process—herein referred to as "transformation of being"—has been known and practiced as meditation for thousands of years by members of esoteric or mystery schools, both East and West.

More specifically this work of transformation has been identified with the inner effort required during meditation. In this paper the term "meditation" is used very broadly to describe a variety of apparently diverse activities—such as Tai Chi, sacred dance, self-remembering, prayer and zazen—which have in common *the intentional focus of attention on the sense of one's being in the present moment.* Through this process the attention itself broadens and allows for deeper experience of being.

Although these practices do have individual development as an aim, they also have the broader purpose of transforming energy to a more refined and higher vibrational state. This perspective invites questions. What is the purpose of all this? In what way does this type of human activity, occurring in the moment of inner work, contribute toward the total balance and harmony of energy transformation in the Universe?

According to G.I. Gurdjieff (Ouspensky, 1949), esoteric tradition describes the Universe as a self-contained system in which two fundamental processes—involution and evolution—complement one another, maintaining the harmony of the All. This involutionary process is the exhilaration of God, the lowering of energy vibration from the divine into manifestation and materiality. The evolutionary process is the inhalation, the return, the raising of energy vibration to the highest state of pure being.

Transformation of being has been described, especially in relationship to the symbolic meaning of the cross (see Figure 1), as a movement in the spiritual or vertical dimension of reality. Movement downward along this axis (involution) indicates a lowering of vibration, a lower level of being and consciousness, and a less intentional role in the Universe. Movement upward (evolution) is the opposite—higher frequency energy, greater being, deeper consciousness, and more intentionality.

While the involutionary process apparently proceeds mechanically, the evolutionary process does not. *Evolution requires the work* (meditation) *of conscious beings.* Herein lies the human potential of voluntary contribution to the harmony of the Universe.

In summary, work on being serves the purpose of maintaining the overall balance of energy transformation. Thus, those focused on this process are devoting themselves to *universal maintenance.*

Transformation of Form
Figure 2: The Horizontal Dimension

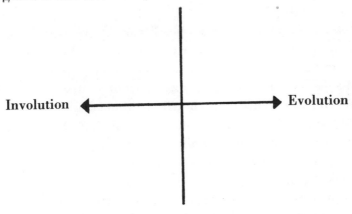

A second transformational process is also described as evolution. This process, which I call "transformation of form," has been the major interest of Western science for the past two hundred years. It is a direct expression of the Western, yang-dominated consciousness seeking to be central in the creative process.

Our educational systems clearly express this interest. The development of the brain's analytic capacities are stressed from early childhood through years of graduate, and even post-graduate, training. Clearly, we in the West are responding to a deeply felt need to have more control over our destiny—to play an active role in the creative aspect of evolution.

Especially during this century the focus on transformation of form is evident in psychological research concerned with self-development. Great efforts have been made toward learning to alter both environmental and inner conditions so that the individual becomes something different—a new person. During the past twenty years, humanistic psychology has specifically focused on just this question (McWaters, 1977). Thus, in this context, the term transformation refers to an alteration in the form of something or someone so as to create a new entity—something that functions or serves a purpose in a manner never before actualized.

Referring again to the cross (see Figure 2), transformation of form is symbolized by the horizontal axis—evolution in time. Movement to the left indicates a degeneration of internal order and a decrease in functionality as a part of a larger whole. The degeneration of a normally contributing member of society to a condition of criminality demonstrates a shift in this direction. Movement to the right symbolizes an increase in internal integration and harmony, and an increase in functional capacity to serve a larger whole. The process of self-actualization illustrates a shift in this direction as the person grows from a condition of inner conflict and alienation to a state of relative inner harmony and fruitful participation in the social environment.

The use of the term evolution in relation to transformation of form is most clearly evidenced in Teilhard de Chardin's (1965) tracing of human development on the planet Earth. Teilhard

notes three nodal points in the evolutionary development of
contemporary humanity—the appearance of matter, life and
thought. He projects that we are infallibly approaching a
further evolutionary transition—the emergence of a conscious
human spirit. This spirit is seen as an entirely new manifestation on the very crest of creative evolution in time.

Work along the horizontal axis serves to generate new forms
or entities, contributing to the cutting edge of growth in the
manifest world. Those focused on this process are devoting
themselves to *universal growth*.

Conscious Evolution
Figure 3

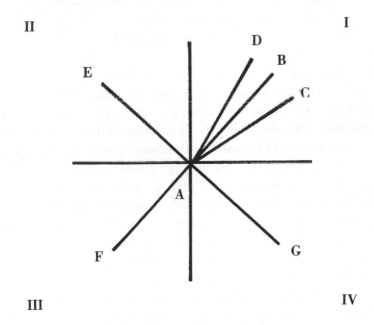

Now to return to the concept of conscious evolution which
synthesizes the two previously discussed modes of transformation. **A conscious individual may choose to serve the
whole, both by the transformation of energy through the**

concentration of attention and by the development of new levels or forms of organization. This synthesis, characteristic of the Aquarian Age, was the goal and focus of Sri Aurobindo's life work.

> Out of the union of these two ideals—the mystic ideal of divine manifestation in life and society and the Western evolutionary ideal of active participation in history—was born the central concept of Integral Yoga, with its emphasis on psychocosmic integration. It is the ideal of illumined cooperation with the spirit of history on the basis of a comprehensive realization of Being as the unity of evolutionary time and the timeless beacon of cosmic awareness.
>
> (Chaudhuri, 1977)

On the individual level, this synthesizing activity of conscious evolution implies two complementary foci. On the one hand, the student learns an appropriate practice of meditation and, over time, develops more fully the ability to focus attention and thereby to transform energy. On the other hand, the student studies himself and works toward untangling neurotic, non-productive behavior, attitudes and belief patterns. Eventually he is able to transform himself into a more harmonious, healthy and conscious person. Given the development of the ability to work in both dimensions, the individual eventually becomes capable of a new level of work. He can now choicefully participate in the transformation of reality.

Returning to the symbolic cross (see Figure 3) we see that attention directed to this twofold path is represented by the diagonal vector AB. This vector represents a balanced participation in conscious evolution.

An intense, yet non-exclusive interest in the transformation of being is symbolized by the more vertical vector AD. Each of these types of activity depicted in quadrant I constitutes a meaningful contribution to conscious evolution.

Speculating about those types of activity symbolized by movement in quadrants II, III and IV is interesting. For example, vector AE might express an intense meditative practice with inadequate regard for social consequences. This may have occurred in certain phases of the Inquisition, with a vehement interest in service to God and with an equally vehement denial of human rights. This illustrates emphasis on the whole, without regard for the part.

Vector AG might denote an overemphasis on social or environmental manipulation and control at the expense of spiritual understanding and work. In the United States and other modern nations, accelerated technological development during the first half of this century has resulted in an improvement in outer conditions accompanied by a degeneration of the inner quality of life. This indicates emphasis on the part (outer conditions of human life) with disregard for the (transpersonal) whole.

This leaves vector AF. It apparently symbolizes what has traditionally been referred to as evil—a force or activity resulting in both a lowering of the quality of being and a degeneration in the general level of life organization. This of course represents the opposite of evolutionary service.

With regard to conscious evolution, it is important to note that the choice to serve in this way becomes possible only at a certain stage of development. At this level the individual has attained a unified and comprehensive self-consciousness and has become aware of his place and potential role in the world.

By analogy, we may now speculate as to the developmental stage at which the Human Being (Humanity, as an organic entity) finds itself. The Human Being is just awakening to the potential for wholeness. Knowing of this potential, we, as individuals, become painfully aware of inner conflict.

Humanity therefore finds itself at the very onset of the therapeutic adventure. How shall we proceed?

For the individual the therapeutic journey begins when a small yet important part of the psyche acknowledges distress and begins to seek help in finding a way of transformation. Initially old behaviors and beliefs persist in customary patterns and defend against change. However, with time and continued effort, the person is eventually able to bring reluctant parts into loving harmony.

Similarly, Humanity begins to recognize the need for healing. We are now seeking help both from the most highly evolved of our race and from the deeper levels of our spiritual nature. As we open and apply ourselves with love, integrity and continuing effort, the Human Being moves toward a self-conscious experience wherein a great meditation and a great transformation occurs. At this stage a work of conscious evolution on a truly profound level becomes possible.

Appendix C
Compendium of Key Concepts

I. A Global Vision

We can voluntarily actualize our potential to discover and nurture transformative thoughts and beliefs, and thereby influence the quality of life on Planet Earth. We can participate in conscious evolution.

The evolution of Humanity is imbued with new meaning when viewed as an experiment in the development of planetary self-consciousness.

We are delightfully tricked to believe that we personally will profit from our quest, but, in the end, we discover our common humanity, our love for Mother Earth, and our intimate need to participate in the living Universe.

We begin to realize that *we are* evolution.

We now begin to enact the great evolutionary experiment wherein the youthful self-consciousness of Gaia finally unites with her ancient intuitive wisdom.

II. What on Earth is Conscious Evolution?

Humanity, rather than stumbling through time, is now being called to ascend to the next intuitional level of consciousness.

If we imagine that Gaia is in her mid-life with another four and a half billion years to go, then we, Humanity, with our ten million years since birth, are equivalent to a two-month-old baby.

Gaia enters the stage of conscious evolution by virtue of the development of her function of self-consciousness—Humanity.

As the parts of myself are recognized as aspects of the whole, conflicting and self-destructive behaviors start to diminish while constructive, integrative qualities ascend.

Experiencing myself in a larger field of influences, I now begin to feel connected to and part of a far greater reality than my personal self could have imagined.

"Evolution" is the development of any type of energy organization or being which progresses to a more conscious and purposeful role in the Universe. "Conscious evolution" is that later phase in evolutionary process wherein the developing entity becomes conscious of itself, aware of the process in which it is involved and begins voluntarily to participate in the work of evolution.

III. We Are What We Think

We simply do not exist except as parts of a larger reality.

All outer reality is born of thought, and we, either unconsciously or consciously, participate in the ongoing creation of the Universe.

Each of us intuitively realizes that we, ourselves, as "children of God," are part of a Universe that unfolds in response to an intention greater than our own.

Clearly the time is ripe to awaken and begin to generate positive evolutionary thoughts that enliven and enlighten our reality.

Rather than seeing outer reality as something to grapple with, we can now choose our dominant modes of thought and perception and thereby influence the reality we experience.

Faith is necessary—faith that thoughts do create reality, faith that we as individuals can change our mode of perception and the quality of our experience, and faith that we, collectively, can influence the process of human and planetary evolution.

IV. Cosmic Glue: Three Metaprinciples

Unity: Everything at every moment exists in living, inter-dependent relationship. Nothing is separate. Everything influences everything else. All is one.

We can if we wish begin to experience our lives as a love affair with the Universe.

Every action, feeling, thought and intuitive insight has a small but definite influence on everything else on the planet. There is no separation. We are part of one being.

Perpetual Transcendence: Within the Universe, there is a coherent system of balanced energy exchange that offers the opportunity for continual transformation into the unknown.

In order to participate consciously in the syntropic evolutionary process, beings must reach a certain level of development wherein they choose to devote their energy to a larger service.

There are no clear-cut guidelines, no rules, only potentials. The results of our exploration and work on the planet will be the test of our capacity for conscious evolutionary service.

Correspondence: The same laws and principles operate analogously on all levels of manifestation. Our ordinary perception binds us to one cosmos, while all the while a multi-dimensional Universe manifests in splendor before, yet invisible to, our very eyes.

V. Becoming Self: Principles of Development

Differentiation: In each evolving being, the parts that are called to play specific, highly specialized roles differentiate to become unique and distinct from one another.

In every organism there seem to be two different lines of development. One serves the involutionary movement of the Universe, the homeostatic/entropic function, while the other serves the evolutionary movement, the transformative/syntropic function. Both are necessary; both are good.

Respect for differentiation can lead us to a deeper understanding of evolutionary process and can allow us to support specialized individuals and groups who explore and develop the mutant consciousness necessary for the leap into an age of conscious evolution.

Integration: In each evolutionary being there is a unification and harmonization of the parts in service of the health and transformation of the whole.

Nucleation: In each evolving being, a center is formed, a center that has in mind: the integrity of the orgamism itself; the establishment of right relationship with the environment; and the transcendent evolution of the orgamism.

We can search for and identify a center within ourselves, and we can choose to become part of the emerging planetary nucleus.

VI. The Fabric of Love: Principles of Relationship

Synergy: A release of free energy can occur when a group of parts or symbiants, inspired by a common aim, join together to form a whole.

The whole is both qualitatively greater and more wonderful than the sum of its parts.

Beyond the capacities of the individual, the group, properly configured, properly supported by its members, and well blessed from above, may be the vehicle for transmitting high-level energies necessary for the emergence of a new age.

Attunement: Deep peace and mutual nurturance can occur when a resonant harmonic relationship is established between an individual evolving being and a greater reality.

Alignment: The wellbeing of all is enhanced when an individual part consciously chooses to serve the evolution of the whole.

The discovery of one's purpose is the rediscovery of a promise made by the soul prior to incarnation.

Quantum Transformation: In each evolving being, the nucleus works toward turning the attention of a significant percentage of the parts toward evolutionary transformation. When this percentage is reached (critical mass), the idea is transmitted rapidly and directly to all parts of the organism, and a quantum evolutionary leap is experienced.

It takes only a clear and definite suggestion from one small part to remind the rest of its inborn preference for evolution.

If a small yet critical percentage of Humanity is able to see the light, there will be intonations and ramifications for all of the human family.

VII. Personal Transformation

Centered around the search for the Self, the second half of life explores and embraces the inner worlds, brings synthesis to a person's understanding, and offers the opportunity for self-initiated conscious evolution.

Psychological wellbeing and growth, however, is a definite challenge for those who wish to evolve. The responsibility of self-transformation rightfully belongs to each of us.

Spiritual realization is a work of opening the attention to that which eternally is.

VIII. Planetary Transformation

The Gaia Hypothesis: Since the very beginning of life on Earth it appears as if the atmosphere has been controlled by something or someone—a self-regulatory intelligence, an evolutionary intention, a guiding wisdom—that has demonstrated its ability by controlling atmospheric conditions in just exactly the way necessary for the survival and evolution of life.

In symbiotic, harmonious relationship with the innate wisdom of Gaia, we, Humanity, will provide a new category of response mechanism, capable of neutralizing the effects of our civilizations on the natural environment and of protecting Gaia, through the use of technology, from unforeseen cosmic threats.

We now enter a period wherein the goal of individual salvation is no longer appropriate. Our guidance calls for a collective transformation. The dispersed elements of the Human Being cry for a self-healing that is guided by deep inner wisdom.

True planetary leadership will emerge only when the glamour of leadership has been transcended, only when holding authority is seen as a sacred function offered in great humility.

IX. Gaia in the Living Universe

Gaia, our Mother Earth, is now preparing for a step forward in evolution. And we, her children, seek to understand the magnificence.

Gaia has now reached the time in her evolutionary cycle when she can let go of her previous function and be transformed to a new and joyful mode of cosmic service.

We are potentially free beings; yet in our current sleep, little is possible. We must first awaken to our subjective, personal self and then to our objective, cosmic Self—which includes the being of Gaia.

Reason and meaning must be wed if ever we are to understand our place and role in the Universe.

X. The Challenge Before Us

We have the means within ourselves, Gaia, the solar system and the Universe to make it all work. Each of us can play a part. Each of us can make a contribution.

Humanity is a great experiment of Divine intention, an adventure in transformation, a seeking, a reaching forward, an exploration into the unknown.

Each of us begins at square one, focusing on physical health, psychological wellbeing and spiritual attunement as preparation for conscious evolutionary service.

We have in our bodies, hearts, minds and spirits the wisdom of the ages. We have at our fingertips all the wonders of modern technology. We have the East and the West, the yin and the yang—infused, informed and guided by the brilliant intention of evolution. The time is here to envision and co-create the adventure of conscious evolution.